'Cheiro' (Count Lou[...]
the greatest seer of m[odern times ...]
uncannily accurate predictions were the date of Queen Victoria's death and the grim destiny that awaited the last Tsar of all the Russias. Cheiro died in 1936.

CHEIRO'S BOOK OF NUMBERS

ARROW BOOKS

Arrow Books Limited
62–65 Chandos Place, London WC2N 4NW

An imprint of Century Hutchinson Limited

London Melbourne Sydney Auckland
Johannesburg and agencies throughout
the world

First published by Herbert Jenkins Ltd
Barrie & Jenkins edition 1978
Arrow edition 1986

This book is sold subject to the condition that it shall not, by way of trade or otherwise, be lent, resold, hired out, or otherwise circulated without the publisher's prior consent in any form of binding or cover other than that in which it is published and without a similar condition including this condition being imposed on the subsequent purchaser.

Printed and bound in Great Britain by
Anchor Brendon Ltd, Tiptree, Essex

ISBN 0 09 948380 7

CONTENTS

CHAPTER		PAGE
	FOREWORD	9
I.	THE PLANETARY NUMBERS OF THE MONTHS. INTRODUCTION TO THE STUDY	30
II.	THE NUMBERS 1 TO 9, CALLED THE "SINGLE" NUMBERS	35
III.	THE NUMBER 1	37
IV.	THE NUMBER 2	40
V.	THE NUMBER 3	43
VI.	THE NUMBER 4	46
VII.	THE NUMBER 5	49
VIII.	THE NUMBER 6	52
IX.	THE NUMBER 7	55
X.	THE NUMBER 8	58
XI.	THE NUMBER 9	64
XII.	THE OCCULT SYMBOLISM OF "COMPOUND" NUMBERS, WITH ILLUSTRATIONS	69
XIII.	THE "COMPOUND" OR "SPIRITUAL" NUMBERS FULLY DESCRIBED	78
XIV.	MORE INFORMATION ON HOW TO USE "SINGLE" AND "COMPOUND" NUMBERS	87
XV.	WHY THE BIRTH NUMBER IS THE MOST IMPORTANT	90
XVI.	SOME ILLUSTRATIONS OF NAMES AND NUMBERS	94
XVII.	EXAMPLES OF HOW NUMBERS RECUR IN LIVES	97
XVIII.	THE DREAD OF THE "13" UNFOUNDED	101
XIX.	EXTRAORDINARY EXAMPLE OF NUMBERS IN THE LIVES OF ST. LOUIS AND LOUIS XVI	106
XX.	PERIODICITY IN NUMBERS	110

CONTENTS (*contd.*)

CHAPTER		PAGE
XXI.	SOME ADDITIONAL INFORMATION	115
XXII.	HOW TO FIND THE "LUCKY" DAY	123
XXIII.	MORE INFORMATION ABOUT COLOURS AND NUMBERS	125
XXIV.	THE VALUE OF CONCENTRATION IN REGARD TO ONE'S NUMBER	128
XXV.	COMBINATIONS BETWEEN 1 HYPHEN 4 PERSONS AND ADVICE TO THOSE BORN UNDER THE NUMBERS 4 AND 8	131
XXVI.	MORE INFORMATION ABOUT PERSONS BORN UNDER THE NUMBERS 4 AND 8	133
XXVII.	THE AFFINITY OF COLOURS AND NUMBERS AND HOW MUSIC AND NUMBERS ARE ASSOCIATED	137
XXVIII.	NUMBER AND DISEASE. PLANETARY SIGNIFICANCE OF HERBAL CURES	140
XXIX.	HOW TO KNOW WHAT CITY, TOWN OR PLACE IS FORTUNATE FOR ONE TO LIVE IN	146
XXX.	HORSE-RACING AND NUMBERS	152
XXXI.	EXAMPLES FROM THE NAMES OF SOME PRESIDENTS OF THE UNITED STATES	154
XXXII.	THE BIBLE AND NUMBERS	174
XXXIII.	CONCLUSION	183

ILLUSTRATIONS

	PAGE
THE DIVISIONS OF THE ZODIAC	17
THE SEVEN-POINTED SEAL OF SOLOMON	22
ZODIACAL AFFINITIES	31

FOREWORD

IT naturally follows that if a person should make a special study of any one subject, from long experience, cultivation and studious research, he will in the end unravel, at least to some extent, the so-called mysteries of the subject on which he has so concentrated his attention.

To the student of Art, Art reveals her mysteries of colour, form, design, pose, and a thousand and one subtleties that escape the ordinary observer. To the student of Biology every leaf tells its own story, every tree its age, every flower its own pedigree.

To the student of Science, what is magic to the uninitiated becomes a natural phenomenon with general laws, governed by rules or calculations that all who choose can learn and understand.

In presenting this book to the public I need then offer no other apology for so doing, than that of having been a student of this particular branch of thought for a very long period, and having proved so-called theories by countless experiments and experiences, I feel I am at last in a position to give to the world at large the result of such studies.

It is admitted by all that the occult side of things has been the one side of life the least explored or investigated. That there is an occult or hidden part in actual relation to human life is on every side a conceded fact, but before this mystery—the greatest of all—the majority of thinkers have held themselves aloof.

In our age the physical and mechanical sciences have called for the greatest attention, yet such things as wireless communication and radium, to-day household words, have been stumbled across by so-called chance.

Already wireless communication has saved hundreds of lives, radium has done likewise, the mysteries of yesterday have become the commonplaces of to-day, and so knowledge in the eternal fitness of things becomes the servant of those who serve.

In pursuit of the laws which have controlled thought in recent centuries, man has, in earning his successes on the physical and mechanical plane, forgotten the loss he has sustained from the lack of study and observation on the occult or psychic side of humanity. He is more occupied to-day in building implements for the destruction of life than he is in the problems of life itself, or in the finding out of those laws which create, control, and sustain life.

When Newton discovered gravitation, it was not supposed for a moment that he had solved the problem of the spheres, and it is sometimes forgotten that when he came to realise that beyond our system of stars, sun, moon and planets there were again the "fixed stars" with their countless systems, in the magnitude of the problem, he could only decide that there was again some occult law behind all, greater than any known law that could even be imagined.

With these few words as a preface, I will endeavour to make my theory so clear that I hope anyone of ordinary intelligence may be able to follow and experiment with certain rules which will be treated in the following chapters.

During my earlier years, when travelling in the East, it had been my good fortune to come in contact with a certain sect of Brahmins who had kept in their hands from almost prehistoric times studies and practices of an occult nature which they regarded as sacredly as they did their own religious teachings. Among other things, they permitted me to learn certain theories on the occult significance of numbers and their influence and relation to human life, which subsequent years and manifold experiences not only confirmed, but justified me in endeavouring to apply them in a practical sense so that others might also use this knowledge with, I hope, advantage to themselves and to those around them.

The ancient Hindu searchers after Nature's laws, it must be remembered, were in former years masters of all such studies, but in transmitting their knowledge to their descendants, they so endeavoured to hide their secrets from the common people that in most cases the key to the problem became lost, and the truth that had been discovered became buried in the dust of superstition and charlatanism, to be re-formed, let us hope, when some similar cycle of thought in its own appointed time will again claim attention to this side of nature.

This ancient people, together with the Chaldeans and Egyptians, were the absolute masters of the occult or hidden meaning of numbers, in their application to time and in their relation to human life.

When examining such questions, we must not forget that it was the Hindus who discovered what is known as the precession of the Equinoxes, and in their calculation such an occurrence takes place every 25,827 years; our modern science after labours of hundreds of years has simply proved them to be correct.

How, or by what means they were able to arrive at such a calculation, has never been discovered—observations lasting over such a period of time are hardly admissible, and calculation without instruments is also scarcely conceivable, and so science has only been able, first to accept their statement, and later to acknowledge its accuracy.

Their judgment, together with that of the Chaldeans, as to the length of what is now known as the cycle of years of the planets, has been handed down to us from the most remote ages, and also by our modern appliances has been proved correct, so when one comes to a study such as this, as to the value of the numbers 1 to 9, which, as the seven harmonies of music are the bases of all music that has ever been conceived, these above-stated numbers are the basis of *all our numbers and calculations*, it is then only logical to accept the decisions of those great students of long past ages and at least examine their deductions with a mind free from bias and prejudice.

It is impossible in a book of this size to give in detail all the reasonings and examples that exist for a belief in the occult side of numbers, but it may interest my readers if I give a few illustrations of why the number 7 has for ages been regarded as *the number of mystery relating to the spiritual side of things*, and why the number 9 has in its turn come to be regarded as the *finality or end of the series on which all our materialistic calculations are built*, but the most casual observer can only admit that beyond the number 9 all ordinary numbers become but a mere repetition of the first 9. A simple illustration of this will readily suffice. The number 10, as the zero is not a number, becomes a repetition of the number 1. The number 11 added together as the ancient occultists laid down in their law of *natural addition*, namely, adding together from left to right, repeats the number 2, 12 repeats 3, 13 repeats 4, and so on up to 19, which in its turn becomes 1 plus 9 equals 10, and so again the repetition of 1. 20 represents 2, and so on to infinity. The occult symbolism of what are called compound numbers, that is, those numbers from 10 onwards, I will explain later.

In this way it will be seen that in all our *materialistic* systems of numbers, the numbers 1 to 9 are the base on which we are compelled to build, just as in the same way the seven great or primary harmonies in music are the bases of all music, and again as the seven primary colours are the bases of all our combinations of colours. In passing, it may be remarked that all through the Bible and other sacred books, the "seven," whenever mentioned, always stands in relation to the spiritual or *mysterious God force*, and has a curious significance in this sense whenever employed.

For a few instances of this, take the seven days (or cycles) of the creation as referred to in Genesis:

The seven heavens, so often referred to.

The seven thrones.

The seven seals.

The seven churches.

The seven days' march round the walls of Jericho, when, on "the seventh day," the walls fell, *before that mysterious God force* symbolised in the number of seven. It is also remarkable that there are exactly seven generations from David to the birth of Christ. In Revelation we read of the "seven spirits of God sent forth into all the earth." Ezekiel speaks of "The seven angels of the Lord that go to and fro through the whole earth," which is believed to be a reference to the magnetic influences of the seven creative planets which radiate through the earth.

Again, we have the seven Spirits referred to in the Egyptian religion.

The seven Devas of the Hindus' Bible.

The seven Amschaspands of Persian faith.

The seven Angels of the Chaldeans.

The seven Sephiroth of the Hebrew Cabala.

The seven Archangels of Revelation, etc. etc.

Let us now take another view of this strange number. If we were to examine every class of occult teaching from the Hindu, Chinese, Egyptian, Greek, Hebrew, or modern school, whichever one may choose, in every case—and without a single exception—we shall find that the quality of the number 7 stands for the expression of that mysterious God force in Nature before referred to.

In the most ancient rules of occult philosophy we find the rule laid down that the number 7 *is the only number capable of dividing "the number of Eternity,"* and continuing in itself as long as the number representing Eternity lasts, and yet, *at every addition of itself producing the number* 9, or in other words it produces the basic number on which all materialistic calculations are built and on which all human beings depend and the whole edifice of human thought finds expression.

EXAMPLE

The number 1 is the first number. It represents the First Cause, Creator, God or Spirit, call it as you like. A circle or the zero, "o," has always been taken as the symbol of endlessness—otherwise Eternity. Place the 1 and the figure zero by its side, and you get the significant symbol of eternity such as 1 plus 0, the 10, and then, place as many of these emblems of eternity side by side as you like, and you get such a figure as 1,000,000. Divide by the mystic number 7 and you get the number 142857.

$$7 \overline{)1,000,000} \\ 142857.$$

Add as many zeros as you like, and keep on dividing by the 7, and you yourself may go on through all eternity and you can only get repetitions of the same 142857, which from time immemorial has been called the "sacred number." Now add this number wherever you find it by natural addition, it will give you the figure 27, and as you have seen by the rule of natural addition described on a preceding page, you keep adding till only one number remains, to arrive at what is known as "the root of the number." You add again 27 by natural addition, and 2 plus 7 equals 9, or in other words, you get the full range of the first series of numbers on which all *materialistic or human calculations can be built*.

Now, let us return to the symbolism of seven for a moment. You know, of course, that Buddha is always represented as sitting in the centre of a Lotus. Let us examine, then, the secret of such a selection. It is not perhaps generally known that the 7 is reproduced in many strange ways in Nature herself, and that flowers that have *not been crossed* by intermingling with other flowers have their outside petals in the number of seven, but as flowers are so easily crossed with other varieties, and it is so difficult to find a pure type, Buddha took the Lotus, which never becomes crossed or loses its individuality, as the emblem of the religion he taught, because, first, its seven foundation petals are always in evidence, and further, the religion he taught was that the creative Spirit was the foundation and origin of all things, and thus again bore silent but unmistakable testimony to the creative action of the seven planets from which all religions have had their origin.

Long before man made his creeds, or civilisations their laws, the influence of these seven planets had become known on the earth. Out of the dark night of antiquity their light became law, and as far as we can penetrate, even to the very confines of prehistoric days, in all races, in all countries, we find the influence of the seven planets through all and in all.

DAYS OF THE WEEK

The seven days of the week have been the outcome of the influence of the seven creative planets and gave the names of the days of the week, in every land or clime. Take any nation you may choose, this fact remains the same, and is so expressed in almost every language, Chinese, Assyrian, Hindu, Egyptian, Hebrew, Greek, Latin, French, German, or English. In modern languages Monday or Moonsday in English becomes Montag in German or Lundi (Lune) in French, Lunes in Spanish, and so on until one comes to Saturday or Saturn's day, the day on which God ordered the Hebrews that no work should be done, and in giving them this command He said, "It is a sign between Me and the children of Israel for ever."[1] And, strange as it may seem, Saturday, year by year, in our modern civilisation is becoming more and more a day of rest.

In connection with this thought, it is worthy of remark that Saturn, the last planet in the series of the seven creative planets of our solar system, in all religions, Hebrew or otherwise, represents "cessation," or rest from labour in another sense. In this strange example one can see the connection between the seven days of the week and the seven creative planets, and it throws a new light on the verse, "God made the sun, moon and stars and appointed them *for signs and for seasons and for days and for years.*" Even Mr. Maunder, the eminent author of so many works on astronomy, calls attention to this strange division of the week into seven days when he says in his *Astronomy of the Bible*: "the period of seven days does not fit precisely into either months or seasons of the year. It is not a division of time *that man would naturally adopt*, it runs across all natural division of time," but this author, not seeing

---

[1] Wherever the Jews went they obeyed this command, even causing their Roman conquerors and other pagan nations to follow their example. Josephus wrote: "There is not a city of the Grecians, nor any of the barbarians, nor any nation whatsoever, whither our custom of resting on the seventh day hath not come."

The seventh day of the Jews is Saturday, called the Sabbath from the Hebrew word Sabbath—to rest.

or perhaps knowing the great hidden truth contained in the number 7, worried only over the point, that it was not "a division of time *which man would naturally adopt.*" But as everything on the earth and above the earth has its meaning, and especially its secret or soul meaning, its place, position, and number, in the "order of things," which is the highest form of design, *every day of the week, every hour of the day, and every minute of the hour, has both its meaning and number*.

It is invariably conceded by every class of scientist that the regularity, order, and system of the wonderful machinery of the heavens is beyond all comparison.

We know to-day that the heavenly bodies move through their orbits with such precision that in millions of years they do not vary one minute of time. We know that they exercise an influence on this earth which is felt by the veriest atoms in the earth, though what this force is, or with what incredible speed it acts, may forever remain a mystery. It was in dealing with this mysterious law that the ancient philosophers by study, experiments, concentration of mind, and perhaps intuition, arrived at the fixation of certain laws governing life, which may be as accurate as their discovery that the "precession of the Equinoxes takes place once in every 25,827 years."

It is from these wonderful students of Nature that we have received the first idea as to the divisions of the Zodiac into twelve periods of 30 degrees, and further, that each period produces a definite and well-known influence on the earth and on human beings born in any of its twelve periods. They further subdivided these 30-degree periods into divisions of three periods of 10 degrees each, in which the planets are also found to have an influence, and they pursued their investigations until they worked out a system demonstrating that each day had its own particular meaning due to vibrations in the ether, which keeps the earth in instantaneous report with its entire solar system, and lastly, that as the sun enters a new degree of the Zodiac in midwinter at about the rate of every $2\frac{1}{2}$ to 3 minutes, and in summer at the rate of 3 to $4\frac{3}{4}$ minutes, that its magnetic

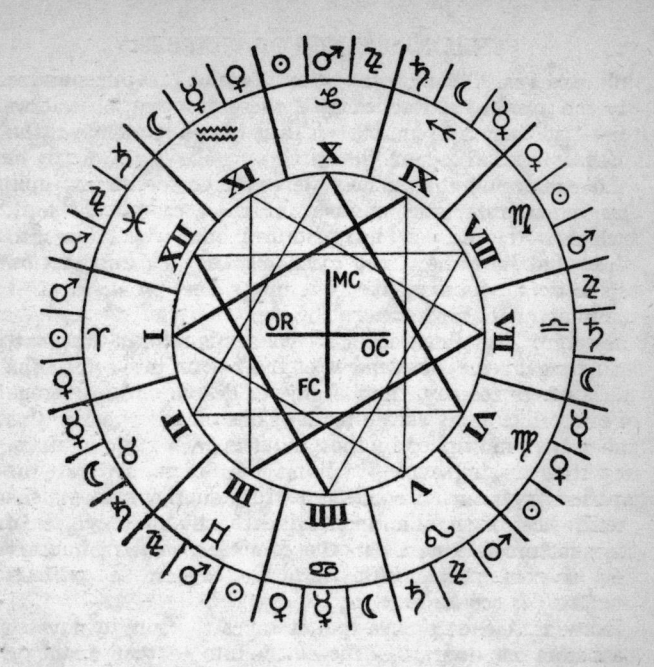

Map showing the Twelve Divisions of the Zodiac, each division subdivided into three parts of 10 degrees.

SIGNS OF THE ZODIAC	SIGNS OF THE SEVEN PLANETS
I. Aries, the Ram	☉ The Sun
II. Taurus, the Bull	♀ Venus
III. Gemini, the Twins	☿ Mercury
IIII. Cancer, the Crab	☽ Moon
V. Leo, the Lion	♄ Saturn
VI. Virgo, the Virgin	♃ Jupiter
VII. Libra, the Balance	♂ Mars
VIII. Scorpio, the Scorpion	
IX. Sagittarius, the Archer	
X. Capricorn, the Goat	
XI. Aquarius, the Water-Bearer	
XII. Pisces, the Fishes	

This map represents the Sun's entry into Aries in the Vernal equinox on March 21–23 of every year. The letters at the points of the central cross stand for: OR—Oriental or Eastern; MC—Mid-Heaven; OC—Occidental or Western; FC—Lower Heaven.

influence varied the effect of the vibrations or ether waves of each planet, and so enabled these students of Nature to carry their system in this way down to almost the smallest fraction of time.[1]

In examining this subject, let us take for an example any remarkable piece of mechanism we may have seen, such as a clock. We have noticed how wheel fits into wheel and how the entire mechanism is put into motion as the ray or tooth of the governing wheel presses against the tooth of the next, and so on.

Keeping this illustration in your mind for a moment, let us regard the 360 degrees of the Zodiac into which the sun appears to pass, from degree to degree on an average of every 4 minutes as the teeth of one of our wheels. This 360 degrees multiplied by the 4 minutes gives 1,440 minutes, and this, divided by 60, to bring it to hours, gives us the 24-hour day, which becomes in its turn another spoke in the great wheel of time, and consequently, by the advance of the sun, must bring us to the commencement of another day *under new and distinct influences, and so on until the year itself is completed.*

Now as science proves that it takes the sun 30 days to pass from one division of the Zodiac into another, again we have the illustration of another wheel, as it were, but a still slower one, being put into motion, and consequently with the change in the heavenly mechanism another set of influences are brought to bear upon the earth, and so on until the twelve months of the year have in their turn experienced the influence of the sun in the twelve divisions of the Zodiac.

Let us now return for a moment to the part played by the seven creative planets. No one to-day, I believe, can plead ignorance of the effect of one of these planets, namely the moon, on the earth itself and on the people who inhabit the earth. We all know, or at least have heard, about the effect of the moon on the brain of people mentally unbalanced. We know how it causes tides to rise and fall

---

[1] This applies, of course, to the motion of the sun through the symbolic or cabbalistic Zodiac used in the East.

along our shores, but still perhaps we do not realise that even in the deepest ocean its pull or attraction is so great that it causes hundreds of thousands of tons of dead weight of water to be drawn up by it to such a height as 70 feet in the Bay of Fundy and in the Bristol Channel.

Scientists, like Darwin in England, Flammarion in France, and others in Germany, made the startling discovery that there are actually tides *in the solid earth itself,* which are affected by the attraction of the moon. *What then of the effect of the moon on the brain itself, which contains the most subtle essence and is one of the greatest mysteries known in life?*

Granted that this be admitted, what then of the part played on human nature by the rest of the planets, which are in each individual case far larger than the moon? The following table showing the dimensions of each of the planets will illustrate better than any words I may use this side of the argument.

Diameter of	Mercury	2,000 miles.
,,	the Moon	2,100 ,,
,,	Venus	7,510 ,,
,,	the Earth	7,913 ,,
,,	Mars	4,920 ,,
,,	Jupiter	88,390 ,,
,,	Saturn	71,900 ,,
,,	Uranus	33,000 ,,
,,	Neptune	36,000 ,,
,,	the Sun	860,000 ,,

I ask, is it logical, with such a demonstration before one, to admit the effect of the moon and to deny any effect to the other planets that are in fact so much larger than it?

Let us now return to the important side of the question as regards the rules set forth in this book. You will very naturally ask, how and when were such numbers arrived at that represent the mechanical action or influence of the celestial system on the people of this earth? I could write an entire volume on this side of the question alone, but in the following necessarily condensed pages you will find the general law explained which may be sufficient to elucidate the system contained in the following chapters.

In the first place, the secret or occult significance of numbers was revealed to man so far back in the world's history that the exact place of their discovery has never been recorded, but it suffices to state that if one goes back in one's investigations to the most distant period in the history of any race who made themselves in any degree responsible for such studies, even there one would find that these numbers representing the qualities of the solar system and the basis of all our later forms of calculation existed.

In working out the idea contained in these pages, I have carefully investigated every important form of occultism bearing on this question, but whether it has been Hindu, Egyptian, Chaldean, or Greek, the symbols of these numbers have always appeared the same, and their relation to months, days, hours, and people representing certain numbers, has been more or less alike.

What is called "the secondary numbers" as illustrated on subsequent pages I myself have brought into a practical form, but they have in every case been built up from long investigation and experience extending over many years. Although we may never be able to find out the exact time in past ages when the influence of these numbers was discovered, that is no reason why we should not accept what has been given us by those ancient students. There are many other things we are forced to accept in life from being conscious of their truth, even when we are not able to get back to their birth or beginnings.

The origin of life we know not, but we are none the less conscious that life exists. The balance, poise, and hidden laws governing our own solar system have also never been explained, together with a thousand other things in our everyday life. The very origin of numbers is itself a mystery; yet we are forced to employ them, and as Balzac says, "without them, the whole edifice of our civilisation would fall to pieces."

Perhaps it may have been that in some far-off time in the history of human life, secrets were *revealed to man by his then more close connection with the "God force" that called life into being.* The Bible itself tells us that in a certain age "God walked with man." Perhaps then "the Fall" may have a still greater meaning than that which has been usually ascribed to it.

In some of the most illumined of the Greek philosophers we find such an age described as when "the gods talked with man" and *taught him the mysteries of his creation.*

This idea is borne out all through the teachings of the Bible. We read in its pages that Abraham, Moses, Elijah, and others, "talked with God." The words "The Lord spake unto Moses" occurs over thirty times in the Book of Leviticus alone. A forcible illustration may also be given from the Book of the Wisdom of Solomon, now included in the Apocrypha, where Solomon says:

For God Himself gave me an unerring knowledge of the things that are, to know the constitution of the world, the beginning and the end and middle of times, the alterations of the solstices, the changes of seasons and the positions of the planets, the nature of living creatures and the thoughts of men, all things that are either secret or manifest I learned, for He that is the artificer of all things taught me this wisdom.

I ask, could anything be more forcible or convincing than such a statement, particularly when it is remembered that the true Seal of Solomon was none other than the seven-pointed star which contained the nine numbers which constitute the base of all our calculations, and which is the root of the system of numbers as applied to human life?

Even in our chemistry we have given a number and symbol to all the elements.

Water is	1010	its symbol is	H_2O
Hydrogen	212	,, ,,	H
Oxygen	1030	,, ,,	O
Nitrogen	1969	,, ,,	N
Carbon	1050	,, ,,	C

and so on.

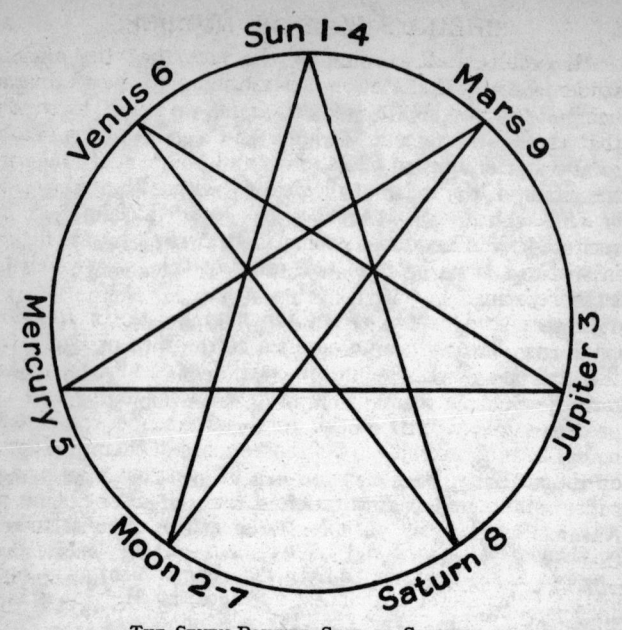

THE SEVEN-POINTED SEAL OF SOLOMON:
EXPLANATION

The Sun, with the numbers 1 hyphen 4, represents the combination of the Sun and the planet Uranus (the male quality of Creation being the Sun with the feminine Uranus *of the mental or spiritual plane*). The Moon, with the numbers 2 hyphen 7, represents the Moon and Neptune, the Moon being feminine on the material or earth plane with Neptune (masculine) *on the mental or spiritual plane*.

The meaning of the lines of the Star being: That Life starts from the Sun—proceeds to the Moon, from that to Mars, from Mars to Mercury, Mercury to Jupiter, Jupiter to Venus, Venus to Saturn, and from Saturn (symbol of death) it returns to the Sun—or God from whence it came—to begin all over again in another cycle, *and so on through eternity.*

All occult studies point to the fact that the ancient students had a foundation for ascribing to every human being *his number in the universe*, and if we admit, as we do, that there is a moment for birth and a moment for death, so also in the links of years, days and hours, that make up the chain of life, it is not illogical to assume that *every link of life has also both its number and place*. I claim that by such a study man may become more perfect by his fitting in with the laws, system, and order of things to which he owes his being.

In this study there is nothing antagonistic to Religion or to our present-day acceptance of the idea of God. On the contrary, man will but honour God the more by his more perfect obedience to Nature's laws. In no text or passage in Holy Writ are we told that God desires human beings to suffer except as the consequence of their own acts; on the contrary, we are everywhere shown that man brings suffering and punishment on himself by his disobedience of Nature's commands. As a logical sequence, it must follow then *that if we move with the laws of life* and *are in harmony with them we must become more happy, healthy, and successful*, and consequently nearer that state of perfection that is the ultimate object of Divine design.

What would you think of a workman in a factory who, instead of moving with the wheels of, say, a weaving machine, attempted to force them in a contrary direction? Would not such a man be crushed, injured, or perhaps lose his life? You would call him a fool, and he would not even gain your sympathy, and if such a man brought such a fatality on himself *by ignorance*, your sentence on him would be perhaps even more severe. Yet you call Nature unjust, cruel, or any other name that may fit into the circumstances —you! *who do not even take the trouble of seeing which way her irresistible forces are moving*. You pray. "Thy will be done on earth as it is in heaven," but you have no more intention of even trying to find out what is the "will" which is obeyed in heaven, and broken by you every second, than if the sacred prayer had never been made.

Your cities are filled with broken lives, your workhouses and mistaken charities are hideous proofs of the failure of your system. Your churches are monuments to the unknown, while *the known lives with you* in every action of your daily life and suffers with you when in your blindness you bring about the evils you could so easily avoid. You have tried every creed, and they have failed to comfort you. You are told to cry that you are "miserable sinners": you are worse, for *you are ignorant sinners*, and it is *your ignorance alone that keeps you miserable*.

How, then, will you accept this thought of another way of looking at life that I bring you in these pages? It may give you a new interest in life. It may yet become a religion unto you, but if it does, it will only unfold the hidden truth of your other religions, the key of whose mysteries you entrusted to priests and prelates, who lost it in their cloisters or buried it in their ceremonies.

To the Jew it will be as precious as to the Christian.

His twelve tribes will live again in the twelve divisions of the Zodiac, in the twelve stones on the breast of the High Priest, and in the building of the Tabernacle. The words he has so often heard, "See that thou makest all things according to the pattern shown thee on the Mount," or in other words the pattern of the heavens carried out in the Temple of Solomon, will now have a true significance in his ears.

He will remember that when his race marched out in triumph from the bondage of Egypt, they did so in four divisions, each carrying a standard *which represented the four divisions of the Zodiac with each of the twelve tribes in their Zodiacal order*.

The Ten Commandments given to Moses on the Mount will no longer represent an unmeaning number, but, as explained by this study, the very number has been chosen to imply by the figure 1, the FIRST CAUSE or the Creator, and the "o"—"the symbol of Eternity." The Ten Commandments were given by the Creator *for all eternity*. They represent the nine planets and the infinity of space beyond, which, like ten steps, lead upward to the farthest boundary of our solar system, beyond which, on the Throne of unimaginable Thought, the Creator of all creates.

Sceptics of Occultism often have the mistaken idea that the ancient astrologers, as they had no sufficiently powerful telescopes, must have been unaware of any planets in our solar system beyond Saturn; but I have shown earlier in these pages that, although they may not have had our wonderful instruments of to-day, yet by some other means they attained a knowledge which equalled, if not outdistanced, our instruments of precision, as, for example, in their discovery of the "precision of the Equinoxes," etc., and in the knowledge of other matters which may have been *revealed* to them in that age when "God talked with man."

There is evidence, however, that those ancient students were conversant with the fact that there were two more distant planets than Saturn in our solar system, for they assigned beyond "the seven creative planets" the orbits for two more heavenly bodies, and they described them as governing the thoughts *on the mental side of Nature* and not the physical, and their description of them is in exact accordance with our present-day knowledge of the effect of the recently discovered planets of Uranus and Neptune on human life.

To the Christian, be he Protestant, Catholic, or Nonconformist, the study, as indicated in these pages, can but increase his faith in the glory of his Creator, and explain much that has hitherto been unexplained and unanswered. He will see in a new light the meaning of the Book of Genesis. The six days' labour, and the seventh—the day of rest—will now have an added interest in his eyes.

He will observe the special selection of the number 12, to be the number of the disciples of Christ, and the anxiety after the death of Judas that the gap should be filled and again the number 12 completed, will now have a more real meaning than it ever had before in its bearing on the twelve periods of the Zodiac. The death of Christ "*as the sun went down on a Friday*," has also in the light of this study a fitness and a meaning which up to now may have been overlooked. In the Book of Genesis we are told that "God rested from His work on the seventh day." Now the seventh day, Saturday, is the symbol of Saturn, *the last of the "seven creative planets"* and itself the symbol of "rest from labour" resignation to the trials and toils of life—or death—whichever way you like to employ the symbol. So in the eternal fitness of things Christ also fulfilled this symbol by stopping His work at such a moment, and passing into the shadow of death as the sun went down at His crucifixion, and the period of Saturn commenced.

"On the first day of the week, at the breaking of the day," again fulfilling the meaning of the "seven creative planets," at the very moment on that day, Sunday, which symbolises the Sun, Christ Himself, called the Sun of Righteousness, rose from the tomb, even as the Ruler of our solar system rose at the same moment from the shadows of the night.

In a thousand and one ways this study demonstrates that the true secret of all religion and all life may be found in the laws of Nature which I have indicated and alluded to in these pages. But, as in this practical age the proof must be by its successful application to the affairs of everyday life, it is to accomplish this that I have worked for years to endeavour so to apply these studies in such a simple way, that any person, even those who have not the slightest knowledge of occultism in any form, may be able to use the system given in this book, and, by a practical application of it to the most ordinary things of everyday life, be so convinced of its truth that they may in the end make it the foundation of all their actions.

The business man need only experiment with it for a few months, when he will be forced to notice how easily things turn for him *on his day*, he will be struck with the strange fact that under his "fortunate numbers" things will be favourable for his plans or for his business; and how much more force or magnetism he will have at each of those periods of the year that come under *his own number*, and especially so on *his own day*. He will begin to notice how curiously the worst days of the week have been those whose numbers he now sees were not in accord with "his number."

He will notice also that the same law applies to his own vitality and health, how he has felt "down" at certain periods of the year, which he will also notice came regularly when he has not been within the "favourable periods" indicated for him.

Ultimately, if he is not a stupid man or simply so narrow-minded or prejudiced that "even if an angel came down from heaven he would not believe," he will begin to apply the rules of this book to all his actions, he will no longer make appointments at random, but will begin to *choose the days* on which he will draw up his contracts, etc. He will then begin to notice *how much easier the machinery of his business works*, he will no longer be the shuttlecock of what before he called "chance," he will no longer "lose his head" or be frightened when worries appear to come in from every side. Now he will expect *them at certain periods, and he will make his plans accordingly*.

In a little time he will notice how much more successful he has become, and how, *with less effort in every sense, more has been accomplished*. He will then begin to apply the same rules to his home, and will see to his amazement how similarly they act. There will no longer be those disputes that there used to be when he *had nothing to guide him*. He will know why to expect those moments of depression and irritability, when the woman he loves persists in telling him that everything is going wrong. He will no longer seek solace at his club. Instead, he will quietly remember that "her numbers" do not accord with the day or perhaps with his own, and will put off the discussion and "the storm" until one of those "favourable periods" which have so often helped him, and as the same magical result takes place with the same regularity and order that it did previously, he is tempted to throw open the window, and looking out into the night and upwards toward the Infinite, he, for the first time, perhaps, will acknowledge that from the smallest action to the greatest, *the same law applies*, and proves the truth that the God who controls to a second of time the movements of millions of worlds *regulates also the actions of man*.

To the most unsuccessful this system will bring success, to the already successful it will bring further success, and to one and all it will bring a new interest in life, and *a higher conception of life itself*.

After upwards of fifty years' study of this subject, and after thousands of experiences and experiments, I am so convinced of the truth of what I give in these pages, that I only ask you but to give these rules a fair trial, and I am certain that you will no longer ascribe the course of your life to "chance"—to do so is to insult your Creator.

Up to now the difficulty has been that so few have endeavoured to reduce what is called Occultism to a practical everyday application. No one before has attempted to translate or interpret into "language understood of the people" the mystical symbolism of such studies.

To this end I have worked, and if I may judge by the number of letters I have received from those who have tried to follow my teachings, I feel I have reason to hope that I have not laboured in vain. The following are a few extracts from letters I have received which help to demonstrate that the truth contained in this study appeals to all classes and conditions of people.

The Rev. W. L. Davidson, D.D., Superintendent of Instruction of the Chatauqua Organisation (U.S.A.), wrote:

Cheiro has so completely converted me by the extraordinary accuracy of his system that I am compelled to forego my scepticism and am determined to study further along these lines of thought.

J. Hart Brougham wrote:

I owe my life's success to what Cheiro has taught me.

J. B. Harvey, late Assistant Attorney-General of the U.S. Government, wrote:

The revelations made by your system are so extraordinarily accurate that they compel belief.

Mrs. J. W. Chapman says:

My life was a continual maze of mistakes until you unfolded to me this system of numbers. Since I commenced to apply it, all has changed, and I am to-day, instead of the failure I was, a successful woman even in a worldly sense, and a happy woman in my home life.

J. W. B., London, writes:

Your system of numbers has been tested by me for months, during my regular business operations. At first I only regarded the favourable and unfavourable periods and days you indicated with curiosity; finally, observation has shown me that these periods were so absolutely exact, that they compelled not only my belief, but my acceptance of your theories to such an extent that I now never make an important appointment without seeing if the date accords with my numbers.

These few extracts from widely differing classes will, I hope, be sufficient to show that, strange though such a study may seem at first, it can be practically demonstrated in everyday life and by all grades and conditions of humanity, and in each case it makes towards the greater fulfilment of life by the betterment, success, and happiness of all who will but follow the rules laid down in these pages.

I am offering to those who may read this book the results of long experience—of many years of patient endeavour. I am convinced that if they will but put my teachings to the test theirs will be that Heritage of Success which is the right of every human being who endeavours by the pursuit of knowledge to make himself more perfect.

"CHEIRO."

CHAPTER I

THE PLANETARY NUMBERS OF THE MONTHS

ALTHOUGH later in these pages the reader will find how the single and compound numbers have each their particular meaning in connection with human life, it is well at this stage to understand how and why the months have received their particular numbers.

The true solar year commences with the Sun's entrance into the Vernal or Spring Equinox on the 21st to the 23rd day of March of every year, and appears to pass through each Sign of the Zodiac of 30 degrees each, one after the other, taking slightly under 365¼ days in so doing, making our year popularly accepted as 365 days.

The Earth, revolving once upon its own axis in each 24 hours, causes the whole of the 13 Signs of the Zodiac in their turn to pass over each portion of the Earth once each 24 hours. The Moon revolves round the earth in a lunar month of 28 days. This wonderful mechanism, if I may call it so, is exactly like the hour-hand, minute-hand and second-hand of a clock.

What is called the first sign of the Zodiac is the "period of the number 9" or the Zodiacal *Sign of ARIES*, from the 21st March to the 19th April. It is ruled by the Planet Mars in its *positive* aspect, and has the 9 for its number.

The "period of the number 6" is the Zodiacal *Sign of TAURUS* from the 20th April to the 20th May. It is ruled by the Planet Venus in its *positive* aspect, and has the 6 for its number.

The "period of the number 5" is the Zodiacal *Sign of GEMINI*, from the 21st May to the 20th June. It is ruled by the Planet Mercury in its *positive* aspect, and has the 5 for its number.

The "period of the 2 and 7" is the Zodiacal *Sign of CANCER*, from the 21st June to the 20th July. It is ruled

ZODIACAL AFFINITIES

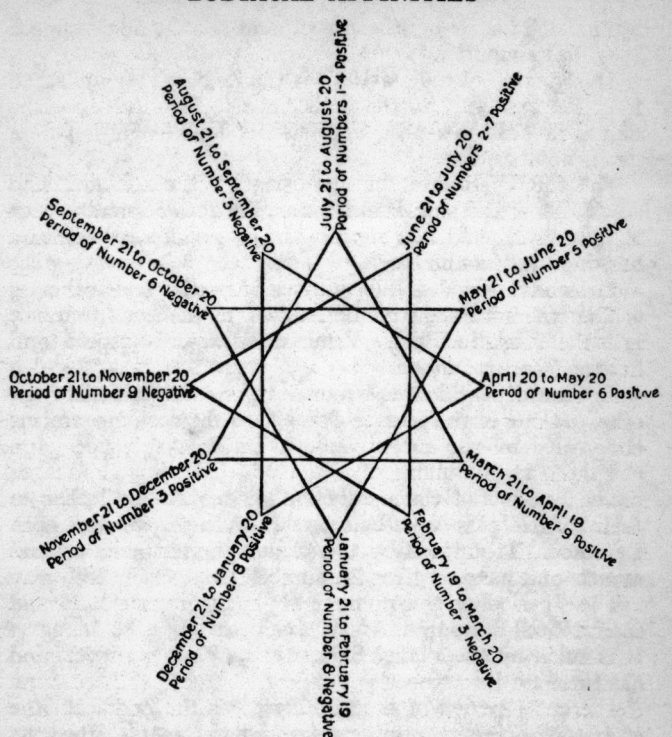

Circular diagram with twelve radiating labels:

- July 21 to August 20 — Period of Numbers 1-4 Positive
- August 21 to September 20 — Period of Number 5 Negative
- September 21 to October 20 — Period of Number 6 Negative
- October 21 to November 20 — Period of Number 9 Negative
- November 21 to December 20 — Period of Number 3 Positive
- December 21 to January 20 — Period of Number 8 Positive
- January 21 to February 19 — Period of Number 8 Negative
- February 19 to March 20 — Period of Number 5 Negative
- March 21 to April 19 — Period of Number 9 Positive
- April 20 to May 20 — Period of Number 6 Positive
- May 21 to June 20 — Period of Number 5 Positive
- June 21 to July 20 — Period of Numbers 2-7 Positive

THE FOUR DIVISIONS OF THE ZODIAC—FIRE, WATER, AIR, EARTH

THE FIRE TRIANGLE
1st "House," March 21 to April 19.
2nd "House," July 21 to August 20.
3rd "House," November 21 to December 20.

THE AIR TRIANGLE
1st "House," May 21 to June 20.
2nd "House," September 21 to October 20.
3rd "House," January 21 to February 19.

THE WATER TRIANGLE
1st "House," June 21 to July 20.
2nd "House," October 21 to November 20.
3rd "House," February 19 to March 20.

THE EARTH TRIANGLE
1st "House," April 20 to May 20.
2nd "House," August 21 to September 20.
3rd "House," December 21 to January 20.

by the Moon in its *positive* aspect, and has the double figure 2—7 for its number.

The "period of the 1 and 4" is the Zodiacal *Sign of LEO*, from the 21st July to the 20th August. It is ruled by the Sun in its *positive* aspect, and has the double figure of 1—4 for its number.

The 2nd "period of the number 5" is the Zodiacal *Sign of VIRGO* from the 21st August to the 20th September. It is ruled by the Planet Mercury in its *negative* aspect, and has the 5 for its number.

The 2nd "period of the number 6" is the Zodiacal *Sign of LIBRA* from the 21st September to the 20th October. It is ruled by the Planet Venus in its *negative* aspect, and has the 6 for its number.

The 2nd "period of the number 9" is the Zodiacal *Sign of SCORPIO* from the 21st October to the 20th November. It is ruled by the Planet Mars in its *negative* aspect, and has the 9 for its number.

The "period of the number 3" is the Zodiacal *Sign of SAGITTARIUS*, from the 21st November to the 20th December. It is ruled by the Planet Jupiter in its *positive* aspect, and has the 3 for its number.

The "period of the number 8" is the Zodiacal *Sign of CAPRICORN*, from the 21st December to the 20th January. It is ruled by the Planet Saturn in its *positive* aspect, and has the 8 for its number.

The 2nd "period of the number 8" is the Zodiacal *Sign of AQUARIUS*, from the 21st January to the 21st February. It is ruled by the Planet Saturn in its *negative* aspect, and has the 8 for its number.

The 2nd "period of the number 3" is the Zodiacal *Sign of PISCES*, from the 19th February to the 20th March. It is ruled by the Planet Jupiter in its *negative* aspect, and has the 3 for its number.

This brings us back to the point from which we started. Owing to the Sun passing from one Sign of the Zodiac to another, seven days are allowed at the beginning of each sign and seven days at the end, which is called the "Cusp of the Sign"; during this period the number of the month and the qualities it represents *are not quite so strong* as during the rest of the period, and partakes to a certain extent *of the qualities of the Sign which is passing away* with those of the one *that is coming into action*.

It will be observed that the Planets have a Positive and Negative quality in accordance with the period of the Zodiac they rule; the Positive giving the more physical and forceful qualities, the Negative the mental.

For example, the symbol of the 9 *positive* in the Sign of Aries is: A man in armour with his visor closed and a naked sword in his hand.

The 9 *negative* in the Sign of Scorpio is represented by a man also in armour, but with the visor up showing his face, and the sword in its sheath, giving the picture of the mental warrior rather than the physical.

THE NUMBERS GIVEN TO THE DAYS OF THE WEEK ARE AS FOLLOWS:

Sunday	1—4
Monday	2—7
Tuesday	9
Wednesday	5
Thursday	3
Friday	6
Saturday	8

These numbers correspond to the Planets as follows:

Sun	1
Moon	2
Jupiter	3
Uranus	4
Mercury	5
Venus	6
Neptune	7
Saturn	8
Mars	9

The Sun and the Moon are the only two Planets having what is called "double numbers," because the Sun and

Uranus are interrelated one to another, so the number of the Sun is written as 1—4.

The Moon being interrelated with Neptune is written as 2—7.

A curious thing, and one well worth noting, is that there appears to be a sympathy and attraction between the numbers 1—4 and 2—7, and it will be found that persons born under any of the 1—4 numbers, such as the 1st, 4th, 10th, 13th, 19th, 22nd, 28th and 31st, are sympathetic and get on well with people born under the numbers 2—7, such as the 2nd, 7th, 11th, 16th, 20th, 25th, and 29th and more especially so if either of these two sets of people is born in the "House of the Moon," namely, between the 20th June and July 21st–27th, or in the "House of the Sun," between the 21st July and August 20th–27th.[1]

[1] NOTE.—I have added the seven days of the "Cusp" to each of thes periods.

CHAPTER II

THE NUMBERS 1 TO 9, CALLED THE SINGLE NUMBERS; HOW THEY INFLUENCE MEN AND WOMEN, TOGETHER WITH THEIR HIDDEN MEANING, AND THE CHARACTER OF PERSONS INDICATED BY THEM

THERE is no getting away from the fact that there are only nine Planets in our Solar System, also that *there are only nine numbers by which all our calculations on this earth are made.* Beyond these nine numbers all the rest are repetitions, as 10 is a 1 with a zero added, an 11 is 1 plus 1, a 2; a 12 is 1 plus 2, a 3; and so on; every number, no matter how high, can be reduced to a single figure by what is called "natural addition" from *left to right*. The final single number that remains is called the "spirit or soul number" of all the previous numbers added together.

In this first part of this study there are only nine numbers to be considered, and one has but to master the occult meaning of each of these nine numbers as they occur in the Birth dates of men and women to find a Key to secrets of human nature that open a source of amazing interest.

I will endeavour to write as simply as possible that all who read may clearly understand what these numbers mean, even in the most everyday actions of life.

Without going into any elaborate description of why this or that influence has been given to any particular number, I will without more preamble go straight to the subject, and show how each person may find what their number may be and how they may utilise this information.

The nine numbers we have got to study are: 1, 2, 3, 4, 5, 6, 7, 8, and 9. These numbers were given to the Planets that control our system in the most distant ages of civilisation, and have been used and adopted by all students of occultism, Chaldean, Hindu, Egyptian, or Hebrew.

The secret underlying the whole of this idea is that of the mysterious law of vibration. The day of Birth giving a Key number that is related to the Planet bearing the same number, this representing a vibration that lasts all through life, and which may, or may not, be in accord with the "Name number," which I will explain later, and with the vibrations of individuals with whom we are brought into contact.

First we must consider each number in relation to the Planet it—if I may use a simple expression—represents.

CHAPTER III

THE NUMBER 1

THE number 1 stands in this symbolism for the Sun. It is the beginning—that by which all the rest of the nine numbers were created. The basis of all numbers is *one*—the basis of all life is *one*. This number represents all that is creative, individual, and positive. Without going into further details, a person born under the Birth number of 1, or any of its series, has the underlying principles of being in his or her work creative, inventive, strongly individual, definite in his or her views, and in consequence more or less obstinate and determined in all they as individuals undertake. This relates to all men and women born under the number 1, such as on the 1st, 10th, 19th, or 28th of any month (the addition of all these numbers making a 1), but more especially so if they happen to be born between the 21st July and the 28th August, which is the period of the Zodiac called the "House of the Sun," or from the 21st March to the 28th April, when the Sun enters the Vernal Equinox and is considered elevated or all-powerful during this period. It is for this reason, which you will observe has a logical basis, that people born under the number 1 in *these particular periods* must have the qualities that I have given to all number 1 people *in a distinctly more marked degree*.

Number 1 people are ambitious; they dislike restraint, they always rise in whatever their profession or occupation may be. They desire to become the heads of whatever their businesses are, and as departmental chiefs they keep their authority and make themselves respected and "looked up to" by their subordinates.

These number 1 people should endeavour to carry out their most important plans and ideas on all days that vibrate to their own number, such as on the 1st, 10th, 19th, or 28th of any month, but especially in those periods

I have described before, namely, from the 21st July to the 28th August, and from the 21st March to the 28th April. Outside of their own numbers, number 1 people get on well with persons born under the 2, 4, and 7, such as those born on the 2nd, 4th, 7th, 11th, 13th, 16th, 20th, 22nd, 25th, 29th, and 31st, especially those born in *the strong periods indicated*.

The days of the week most fortunate for number 1 persons are Sunday and Monday, and especially so if one of their "own numbers" should also fall on that day, such as the 1st, 10th, 19th, or 28th, and next to that their interchangeable numbers of 2, 4, 7, such as the 2nd, 4th, 7th, 11th, 13th, 16th, 20th, 22nd, 25th, 29th, or 31st.

The most fortunate colours for persons born under the number 1 are all shades of gold, yellows and bronze to golden brown.

Their "lucky" jewels are the topaz, amber, yellow diamond and all stones of these colours.

If possible, they should wear a piece of amber next their flesh.

FAMOUS PEOPLE BORN UNDER THE NUMBER 1

Alexander the Great	Born 1st July	Represents a 1
James I	,, 28th June	,, ,, 1
Charles I	,, 19th Nov.	,, ,, 1
George I	,, 28th May	,, ,, 1
George II	,, 10th Oct.	,, ,, 1
Duke of Wellington	,, 1st May	,, ,, 1
General Gordon	,, 28th Jan.	,, ,, 1
President Garfield (U.S.A.)	,, 19th Nov.	,, ,, 1
"General" Booth	,, 10th April	,, ,, 1
Field-Marshal Earl Haig	,, 19th June	,, ,, 1
Queen Alexandra	,, 1st Dec.	,, ,, 1
Field-Marshal Lord French	,, 28th Sept.	,, ,, 1
David Livingstone	,, 19th Mar.	,, ,, 1
Lord Charles Beresford	,, 10th Feb.	,, ,, 1
Annie Besant	,, 1st Oct.	,, ,, 1
President Wilson (U.S.A.)	,, 28th Dec.	,, ,, 1
President Monroe (U.S.A.)	,, 28th April	,, ,, 1
President Hoover (U.S.A.)	,, 10th Aug.	,, ,, 1

CHEIRO'S BOOK OF NUMBERS

Orville Wright (*Flying Machines*)	Born 19th Aug.	Represents a	1
Sven Hedin (*Explorer*)	,, 19th Feb.	,,	,, 1
Chopin (*Composer*)	,, 1st Mar.	,,	,, 1
William Dean Howells (*Author*)	,, 1st Mar.	,,	,, 1
Bismarck	,, 1st April	,,	,, 1
Sir Edwin Arnold (*Author*)	,, 10th June	,,	,, 1
Sir Robert Ball (*Astronomer*)	,, 1st July	,,	,, 1
John Calvin (*Religious Reformer*)	,, 10th July	,,	,, 1
Mary Anderson (*American Actress*)	,, 28th July	,,	,, 1
Alexandre Dumas (*Author*)	,, 28th July	,,	,, 1
Oliver Wendell Holmes (*Author*)	,, 28th Aug.	,,	,, 1
President Adams (U.S.A.)	,, 19th Oct.	,,	,, 1
"Cheiro"	,, 1st Nov.	,,	,, 1
Delcassé (*French Diplomat*)	,, 1st Nov.	,,	,, 1
William Hogarth (*Painter*)	,, 10th Nov.	,,	,, 1
Captain Cook (*Explorer*)	,, 28th Oct.	,,	,, 1
Danton (*French Revolution*)	,, 28th Oct.	,,	,, 1
Goethe	,, 28th Aug.	,,	,, 1
Oliver Goldsmith	,, 10th Nov.	,,	,, 1
Ferdinand de Lesseps (*Engineer*)	,, 19th Nov.	,,	,, 1
Thomas More (*Irish Poet*)	,, 28th May	,,	,, 1
Nansen (*Arctic Explorer*)	,, 10th Oct.	,,	,, 1
Sir Charles Napier	,, 10th Aug.	,,	,, 1
Charles Stewart Parnell	,, 28th June	,,	,, 1
Adelina Patti (*Prima Donna*)	,, 10th Feb.	,,	,, 1
Edgar Allan Poe (*Poet*)	,, 19th Jan.	,,	,, 1
Lord Russell of Killowen	,, 10th Nov.	,,	,, 1
Sir H. M. Stanley (*Explorer*)	,, 28th Jan.	,,	,, 1
Brigham Young (*Mormon Head*)	,, 1st June	,,	,, 1

CHAPTER IV

THE NUMBER 2

THE number 2 stands in symbolism for the Moon. It has the feminine attributes of the Sun, and, for this reason alone, although number 1 and number 2 people are decidedly opposite in their characters, their vibrations are harmonious and they make good combinations.

Number 2 persons are gentle by nature, imaginative, artistic, and romantic. Like the number 1 people, they are also inventive, but they are not as forceful in carrying out their ideas. Their qualities are more *on the mental* than the physical plane and they are seldom as strong physically as those born under the number 1.

Number 2 people are all those who are born on the 2nd, 11th, 20th, or 29th in any month, but their characteristics are the more marked if they are born between the 20th June and the 27th July, this period being what is called the "House of the Moon." I have added the seven days of the "Cusp" to the 20th July.

Number 2 persons and number 1 vibrate together, and in a lesser degree with number 7 people, such as those born on the 7th, 16th, or 25th in any month.

Number 2 persons should endeavour to carry out their chief plans and ideas on days whose numbers vibrate with their own, such as on the 2nd, 11th, 20th, or 29th of any month, but more especially during the period of the 20th June to the 27th July.

The days of the week more fortunate or "lucky" for them are Sunday, Monday, and Friday (the reason Friday is favourable in this case is that it is governed by Venus), and especially so if, like the number 1 people, one of their own numbers should fall on either of these days, such as the 2nd, 11th, 20th, or 29th, and next to these their interchangeable numbers of 1, 4, 7, such as the 1st, 4th, 7th, 10th, 13th, 16th, 19th, 22nd, 25th, 28th, or 31st.

The chief faults they should guard against are—being restless and unsettled, lack of continuity in their plans and ideas, and lack of self-confidence. They are also inclined to be oversensitive, and too easily get despondent and melancholy if they are not in happy surroundings.

For "lucky" colours they should wear all shades of green, from the darkest to the lightest, also cream and white, but as far as possible they should avoid all dark colours, especially black, purple, and dark red.

Their "lucky" stones and jewels are pearls, moonstones, pale green stones, and they should carry a piece of jade always with them, and, if possible, next their skin.

FAMOUS PEOPLE BORN UNDER THE NUMBER 2

Thomas Chatterton, the Boy Poet	Born 20th Nov.	Represents a 2
Swedenborg	,, 29th Jan.	,, ,, 2
Marie Antoinette, Queen of France	,, 2nd Nov.	,, ,, 2
Gladstone	,, 29th Dec.	,, ,, 2
Queen Elizabeth of Rumania (*Poetess*)	,, 29th Dec.	,, ,, 2
Sadi Carnot, President of France	,, 11th Aug.	,, ,, 2
General Boulanger	,, 29th April	,, ,, 2
Napoleon III	,, 20th April	,, ,, 2
King Victor Emmanuel III	,, 11th Nov.	,, ,, 2
Edison	,, 11th Feb.	,, ,, 2
David Garrick (*Actor*)	,, 20th Feb.	,, ,, 2
Lord Curzon of Kedleston	,, 11th Jan.	,, ,, 2
Ibsen (*Author*)	,, 20th Mar.	,, ,, 2
William Lecky (*Historian*)	,, 20th Mar.	,, ,, 2
Charles II	,, 29th May	,, ,, 2
Sir Edward Elgar (*Composer*)	,, 2nd June	,, ,, 2
Thomas Hardy (*Author*)	,, 2nd June	,, ,, 2
Gluck (*Composer*)	,, 2nd July	,, ,, 2
President Adams (U.S.A.)	,, 11th July	,, ,, 2
President Harding (U.S.A.)	,, 2nd Nov.	,, ,, 2
President Poincaré (France)	,, 20th Aug.	,, ,, 2

Paul Bourget (*Author*)	Born	2nd Sept.	Represents a 2
Henry George (*Author*)	,,	2nd Sept.	,, ,, 2
Amelia E. Barr (*Authoress*)	,,	29th Mar.	,, ,, 2
Max O'Rell (*Author*)	,,	2nd Mar.	,, ,, 2
Eugene Field (*Poet*)	,,	2nd Sept.	,, ,, 2
Henry George (*Writer*)	,,	2nd Sept.	,, ,, 2
Joseph Jefferson (*Actor*)	,,	20th Feb.	,, ,, 2
Pope Leo XIII	,,	2nd Mar.	,, ,, 2
Alfred de Musset (*Poet*)	,,	11th Nov.	,, ,, 2
Pope Pius X	,,	2nd June	,, ,, 2

CHAPTER V

THE NUMBER 3

THE number 3 stands in symbolism for the Planet Jupiter, a Planet which plays a most important rôle both in Astrology and in all systems of Numerology. It is the beginning of what may be termed one of the main lines of force that runs right through all the numbers from 3 to 9.

It has a special relation to every third in the series, such as 3, 6, 9, and all their additions. These numbers added together in any direction produce a 9 as their final digit, and the 3, 6, 9 people are all sympathetic to one another.

Persons having a 3 for their Birth number are all those who are born on the 3rd, 12th, 21st, or 30th in any month, but the number 3 has still more significance if they should be born in what is called the "period of the 3," from the 19th February to March 20th–27th, or from the 21st November to December 20th–27th.

Number 3 people, like the number 1 individuals, are decidedly ambitious; they are never satisfied by being in subordinate positions; their aim is to rise in the world, to have control and authority over others. They are excellent in the execution of commands; they love order and discipline in all things; they readily obey orders themselves, but they also insist on having their orders obeyed.

Number 3 people often rise to the very highest positions in any business, profession or sphere in which they may be found. They often excel in positions of authority in the army and navy, in government, and in life generally; and especially in all posts of trust and responsibility, as they are extremely conscientious in carrying out their duties.

Their faults are that they are inclined to be dictatorial, to "lay down the law" and to insist on carrying out their own ideas. For this reason, although they are not quarrelsome, they succeed in making many enemies.

Number 3 people are singularly proud; they dislike being under an obligation to others; they are also exceptionally independent, and chafe under the least restraint.

Number 3 people should endeavour to carry out their plans and aims on all days that vibrate to their own number, such as on the 3rd, 12th, 21st, and 30th of any month, but more especially when these dates fall in the "period of the 3," such as from the 19th February to March 20th–27th, and from the 21st November to December 20th–27th.

The days of the week more "lucky" for them are Thursday, Friday, and Tuesday; Thursday being the most important. These days are especially good if a number making a 3 should fall on it, such as the 3rd, 12th, 21st, or 30th, and next in order their interchangeable numbers of 6 and 9 such as the 6th, 9th, 15th, 18th, 24th, or 27th.

Number 3 people are more in harmony with those born under their own number or under the 6 and 9, such as all those who are born on a

> 3rd, 12th, 21st, 30th.
> 6th, 15th, 24th.
> 9th, 18th, 27th.

For "lucky" colours they should wear some shade of mauve, violet, or purple, or some touch of these colours should always be with them; also in the rooms in which they live. All shades of blue, crimson, and rose are also favourable to them, but more as secondary colours.

Their "lucky" stone is the amethyst. They should always have one on their persons, and, if possible, wear it next their skin.

FAMOUS PEOPLE BORN UNDER THE NUMBER 3

King George V . . .	Born 3rd June	Represents a 3
Emperor Frederick of Germany	,, 21st Nov.	,, ,, 3
Gambetta of Italy . .	,, 30th Oct.	,, ,, 3
Lord Russell . . .	,, 12th Aug.	,, ,, 3

CHEIRO'S BOOK OF NUMBERS

Abraham Lincoln, President U.S.A.	Born 12th Feb.	Represents a 3
Winston Churchill, M.P.	,, 30th Nov.	,, ,, 3
Field-Marshal Lord Roberts, V.C.	,, 30th Sept.	,, ,, 3
Rudyard Kipling	,, 30th Dec.	,, ,, 3
Sir Arthur Sullivan	,, 12th May	,, ,, 3
Sir Charles Hawtrey	,, 21st Sept.	,, ,, 3
Lord Beaconsfield	,, 21st Dec.	,, ,, 3
Darwin (*Naturalist*)	,, 12th Feb.	,, ,, 3
George Pullman (*Pullman cars*)	,, 3rd Mar.	,, ,, 3
Bishop Heber	,, 21st April	,, ,, 3
Sir Alfred Austin (*Poet*)	,, 30th May	,, ,, 3
Richard Cobden (*Free Trade*)	,, 3rd June	,, ,, 3
The Earl of Aberdeen	,, 3rd Aug.	,, ,, 3
King Haakon (*Norway*)	,, 3rd Aug.	,, ,, 3
George IV	,, 12th Aug.	,, ,, 3
The First Lord Oxford and Asquith	,, 12th Sept.	,, ,, 3
William Cullen Bryant (*Poet*)	,, 3rd Nov.	,, ,, 3
Mrs. Craigie (*Authoress*)	,, 3rd Nov.	,, ,, 3
Pope Benedict	,, 21st Nov.	,, ,, 3
"Mark Twain"	,, 30th Nov.	,, ,, 3
President Felix Faure (France)	,, 30th Jan.	,, ,, 3
Mendelssohn (*Composer*)	,, 3rd Feb.	,, ,, 3
Cardinal Newman	,, 21st Feb.	,, ,, 3
Dean Swift	,, 30th Nov.	,, ,, 3
Voltaire	,, 21st Nov.	,, ,, 3
Ramsay MacDonald (*First Labour Prime Minister of England*)	,, 12th Oct.	,, ,, 3

CHAPTER VI

THE NUMBER 4

THE number 4 stands in its symbolism for the Planet Uranus. It is considered related to the Sun, number 1, and in occultism is written as 4—1.

Number 4 people have a distinct character of their own. They appear to view everything from an opposite angle to everyone else. In an argument they will always take the opposite side, and although not meaning to be quarrelsome, yet they bring about opposition and make a great number of secret enemies who constantly work against them.

They seem quite naturally to take a different view of anything that is presented to their minds. They instinctively rebel against rules and regulations, and if they can have their way they reverse the order of things, even in communities and governments. They often rebel against constitutional authority and set up new rules and regulations either in domestic or public life. They are inclined to be attracted to social questions and reforms of all kinds, and are very positive and unconventional in their views and opinions.

Number 4 people are all those who are born on the 4th, 13th, 22nd, and 31st in any month; their individuality is still more pronounced if they are born in the Zodiacal period of the Sun and Moon, namely, between the 21st June and July 20th–27th (Moon period) and from the 21st July to the end of August (Sun period).

Number 4 people do not make friends easily. They seem more attracted to persons born under the 1, 2, 7 and 8 numbers.

They are seldom as successful in worldly or material matters as people born under the other numbers, and as a rule they are more or less indifferent as to the accumulation of wealth. If they do acquire money or have it given to them they generally surprise people by the way they employ it or the use they put it to.

They should endeavour to carry out their plans and ideas on all days that have their number 4, such as the 4th, 13th, 22nd, and 31st of any month, but especially so if these dates come in their strong period, from the 21st June to July 20th–27th, or from the 22nd July to the end of August.

The days of the week more fortunate or "lucky" for them are Saturday, Sunday, and Monday, especially so if their "own number" should fall on one of these days, such as the 4th, 13th, 22nd, or 31st, and next in order their interchangeable numbers of 1, 2, 7, such as the 1st, 2nd, 7th, 10th, 11th, 16th, 19th, 20th, 25th, 28th, or 29th.

Their chief faults are that they are most highly strung and sensitive, very easily wounded in their feelings, inclined to feel lonely and isolated, and are likely to become despondent and melancholy unless they have achieved success. As a rule they make few real friends, but to the few they have, they are most devoted and loyal, but are always inclined to take the part of "the under-dog" in any argument or any cause they espouse.

For "lucky" colours, they should wear what are called "half-shades," "half-tones," or "electric colours." "Electric blues" and greys seem to suit them best of all.

Their "lucky" stone is the sapphire, light or dark, and if possible they should wear this stone next their skin.

FAMOUS PEOPLE BORN UNDER THE NUMBER 4

The Earl of Stafford	Born 13th April	Represents a 4
George Washington	,, 22nd Feb.	,, ,, 4
Lord Byron	,, 22nd Jan.	,, ,, 4
George Eliot	,, 22nd Nov.	,, ,, 4
Lord Baden-Powell of Gilwell	,, 22nd Feb.	,, ,, 4
The Queen of Holland	,, 31st Aug.	,, ,, 4
Sarah Bernhardt	,, 22nd Oct.	,, ,, 4
Thomas Carlyle	,, 4th Dec.	,, ,, 4
Faraday	,, 22nd Oct.	,, ,, 4

Lord Leighton (*Painter*)	Born 4th Dec.	Represents a 4
Prince Charlie ("The Young Pretender")	,, 31st Dec.	,, ,, 4
Sir Francis Bacon (*Philosopher*)	,, 22nd Jan.	,, ,, 4
James Russell Lowell (*Poet*)	,, 22nd Feb.	,, ,, 4
Haydn (*Composer*)	,, 31st April	,, ,, 4
Thomas Huxley (*Philosopher*)	,, 4th May	,, ,, 4
Alphonse Daudet (*Writer*)	,, 13th May	,, ,, 4
Sir Arthur Conan Doyle	,, 22nd May	,, ,, 4
George III	,, 4th June	,, ,, 4
Julian Hawthorne (*Author*)	,, 22nd June	,, ,, 4
Rider Haggard (*Author*)	,, 22nd June	,, ,, 4
General Goettals (*Panama Canal fame*)	,, 22nd June	,, ,, 4
Nathaniel Hawthorne (*Author*)	,, 4th July	,, ,, 4
Emma Eames (*Prima Donna*)	,, 13th Aug.	,, ,, 4
Archbishop Corrigan (*New York*)	,, 13th Aug.	,, ,, 4
Ex-Sultan Abdul Hamid	,, 22nd Sept.	,, ,, 4
Saint Augustine	,, 13th Nov.	,, ,, 4
George Eliot (*Authoress*)	,, 22nd Nov.	,, ,, 4
Heinrich Heine (*Author*)	,, 13th Dec.	,, ,, 4
Immanuel Kant (*Philosopher*)	,, 22nd April	,, ,, 4
Sir Isaac Pitman (*Inventor of Shorthand*)	,, 4th Jan.	,, ,, 4
Pope Pius IX	,, 13th May	,, ,, 4
Russell Sage (*Financier*)	,, 4th Aug.	,, ,, 4
Schubert (*Composer*)	,, 31st Jan.	,, ,, 4
Sir Arthur Sullivan (*Composer*)	,, 13th May	,, ,, 4
Richard Wagner (*Composer*)	,, 22nd May	,, ,, 4
Sir Hamilton Harty	,, 4th Dec.	,, ,, 4

CHAPTER VII

THE NUMBER 5

THE number 5 stands in symbolism for the Planet Mercury, and is versatile and mercurial in all its characteristics.

Number 5 people are all those who are born on the 5th, 14th, and 23rd in any month, but their characteristics are still more marked if they are born in what is called the "period of the 5," which is from the 21st May to June 20th–27th, and from the 21st August to September 20th–27th.

Number 5 people *make friends easily* and get on with persons born under *almost any other number*, but their best friends are those who are born under their own number, such as the 5th, 14th, and 23rd of any month.

Number 5 people are mentally very highly strung. They live on their nerves and appear to crave excitement.

They are quick in thought and decisions, and impulsive in their actions. They detest any plodding kind of work and seem naturally to drift into all methods of making money quickly. They have a keen sense of making money by inventions and new ideas. They are born speculators, prone to Stock Exchange transactions, and generally are willing and ready to run risks in all they undertake.

They have the most wonderful elasticity of character. They rebound quickly from the heaviest blow; nothing seems to affect them for very long; like their symbol, quicksilver, which Mercury represents, the blows of Fate leave no indentations on their character. If they are by nature good they remain so; if bad, not all the preaching in the world will make the slightest effect on them.

Number 5 people should endeavour to carry out their plans and aims on all days that fall under their "own number," such as the 5th, 14th, or 23rd of any month, but more especially when these dates fall in the "period of the 5," namely from the 21st May to June 20th–27th, or from the 21st August to September 20th–27th.

The days of the week more fortunate or "lucky" for them are Wednesday and Friday, especially if their "own number" falls on one of these days.

Their greatest drawback is that they exhaust their nervous strength to such an extent that they often fall victims to nervous breakdowns of the worst kind, and under any mental tension they easily become irritable and quick-tempered, unable to "suffer fools gladly."

Their "lucky" colours are all shades of light grey, white, and glistening materials, but just as they can make friends with people born under all kinds of numbers, so can they wear all shades of colours, but by far the best for them are light shades, and they should wear dark colours as rarely as possible.

Their "lucky" stone is the diamond, and all glittering or shimmering things; also ornaments made of platinum or silver, and, if possible, they should wear a diamond set in platinum next their skin.

FAMOUS PEOPLE BORN UNDER THE NUMBER 5

St. Louis of France	Born 23rd May	Represents a 5
Louis XVI	,, 23rd Aug.	,, ,, 5
Empress Eugénie	,, 5th May	,, ,, 5
H.M. King George VI	,, 14th Dec.	,, ,, 5
H.R.H. The Duke of Windsor	,, 23rd June	,, ,, 5
Samuel Pepys	,, 23rd Feb.	,, ,, 5
Sir Hiram Maxim (*Inventor*)	,, 5th Feb.	,, ,, 5
Lord Lister	,, 5th April	,, ,, 5
T. P. O'Connor, M.P.	,, 5th Oct.	,, ,, 5
Jean de Reske (*Tenor*)	,, 14th Jan.	,, ,, 5
Sir Henry Bessemer (*Inventor*)	,, 14th Mar.	,, ,, 5
Humbert I of Italy	,, 14th Mar.	,, ,, 5
Shakespeare	,, 23rd April	,, ,, 5
Thomas Hood (*Poet*)	,, 23rd May	,, ,, 5
Châteaubriand (*Author*)	,, 14th Sept.	,, ,, 5

Benedict Arnold (*American spy of the Revolution*)	Born 14th Jan.	Represents a 5
Barnum (*of Circus fame*)	,, 5th July	,, ,, 5
Erard (*Inventor of the Grand Piano*)	,, 5th April	,, ,, 5
Handel (*Composer*)	,, 23rd Feb.	,, ,, 5
Fahrenheit (*Inventor*)	,, 14th May	,, ,, 5
Josephine, Queen of France	,, 23rd June	,, ,, 5
Karl Marx (*Socialist*)	,, 5th May	,, ,, 5
Mesmer (*Discoverer of Magnetism*)	,, 23rd May	,, ,, 5
Sir Gilbert Parker (*Author*)	,, 23rd Nov.	,, ,, 5
Cardinal Richelieu	,, 5th Sept.	,, ,, 5
W. T. Stead (*Editor*)	,, 5th Feb.	,, ,, 5
Talleyrand (France)	,, 14th Feb.	,, ,, 5

CHAPTER VIII

THE NUMBER 6

THE number 6 stands in symbolism for the Planet Venus. Persons having a 6 as their Birth number are all those who are born on the 6th, 15th, or 24th of any month, but they are more especially influenced by this number if they are born in what is called the "House of the 6th," which is from the 20th April to May 20th–27th, and from the 21st September to October 20th–27th.

As a rule all number 6 people are extremely magnetic; they attract others to them, and they are loved and often worshipped by those under them.

They are very determined in carrying out their plans, and may, in fact, be deemed obstinate and unyielding, except when they themselves become deeply attached: in such a case they become devoted slaves to those they love.

Although number 6 people are considered influenced by the Planet Venus, yet as a rule theirs is more the "mother love" than the sensual. They lean to the romantic and ideal in all matters of the affections. In some ways they take very strongly after the supposed qualities of Venus, in that they love beautiful things, they make most artistic homes, are fond of rich colours, also paintings, statuary, and music.

If rich they are most generous to art and artists, they love to entertain their friends and make everyone happy about them, but the one thing they cannot stand is discord and jealousy.

When roused by anger they will brook no opposition, and will fight to the death for whatever person or cause they espouse, or out of their sense of duty.

The number 6 people have got the power of making more friends than any other class, with the exception of the number 5, but especially so with all persons born under the vibration of the 3, the 6, the 9, or all their series.

Their most important days in the week are Tuesdays, Thursdays, and Fridays, and especially so if a number of 3, 6, or 9, such as the 3rd, 6th, 9th, 12th, 15th, 18th, 21st, 24th, 27th, or 30th, should fall on one of those days.

Number 6 people should endeavour to carry out their plans and aims on all dates that fall under their "own number," such as the 6th, 15th, or 24th of any month, but more especially when these dates fall in the "period of the 6," namely, between the 20th April and May 20th–27th, or from the 21st September to October 20th–27th.

Their "lucky" colours are all shades of blue, from the lightest to the darkest, also all shades of rose or pink, but they should avoid wearing black or dark purple.

Their "lucky" stone is especially the turquoise, and, as far as possible, they should wear one, or a piece of turquoise matrix, next their skin. Emeralds are also "lucky" for the number 6 people.

FAMOUS PEOPLE BORN UNDER THE NUMBER 6

Queen Victoria of England	Born 24th May	Represents a 6	
Napoleon I	,, 15th Aug.	,, ,, 6	
Frederick the Great	,, 24th Jan.	,, ,, 6	
Duke of Marlborough	,, 24th May	,, ,, 6	
Emperor Maximilian of Mexico	,, 6th July	,, ,, 6	
Henry VI	,, 6th Dec.	,, ,, 6	
Oliver Cromwell	,, 24th April	,, ,, 6	
Cecil Rhodes	,, 6th July	,, ,, 6	
Joan of Arc	,, 6th Jan.	,, ,, 6	
Admiral Lord Jellicoe	,, 6th Dec.	,, ,, 6	
President Taft (U.S.A.)	,, 15th Sept.	,, ,, 6	
Sir Walter Scott	,, 6th Dec.	,, ,, 6	
Sir Henry Irving	,, 6th Feb.	,, ,, 6	
Joseph Choate (*U.S. Ambassador to England*)	,, 24th Jan.	,, ,, 6	
Susan B. Anthony (*Suffragette*)	,, 15th Feb.	,, ,, 6	
Michael Angelo (*Painter*)	,, 6th Mar.	,, ,, 6	
Elizabeth Browning (*Poet*)	,, 6th Mar.	,, ,, 6	

Henry Ward Beecher (*Preacher*)	Born 24th June	Represents a 6
President Diaz (Mexico)	,, 15th Sept.	,, ,, 6
Sir William Herschel (*Astronomer*)	,, 15th Nov.	,, ,, 6
Grace Darling (*Heroine*)	,, 24th Nov.	,, ,, 6
Warren Hastings (*Statesman*)	,, 6th Dec.	,, ,, 6
King George I (Greece)	,, 24th Dec.	,, ,, 6
John Knox (*Reformer*)	,, 24th Nov.	,, ,, 6
Molière (*Author*)	,, 15th Jan.	,, ,, 6
Max Müller (*Philosopher and Poet*)	,, 6th Dec.	,, ,, 6
Daniel O'Connell (*Statesman*)	,, 6th Aug.	,, ,, 6
Count de Paris (Louis Philippe)	,, 24th Aug.	,, ,, 6
Admiral Peary (*North Pole fame*)	,, 6th May	,, ,, 6
Sir Arthur Pinero (*Author*)	,, 24th May	,, ,, 6
Rembrandt (*Painter*)	,, 15th July	,, ,, 6
Alfred Tennyson (*Poet*)	,, 6th Aug.	,, ,, 6
George Westinghouse (*Inventor*)	,, 6th Oct.	,, ,, 6

CHAPTER IX

THE NUMBER 7

THE number 7 stands in symbolism for the Planet Neptune, and represents all persons born under the 7, namely those who are born on the 7th, 16th, or 25th of any month, but more especially influences such persons if they were born from the 21st June to July 20th–27th, the period of the Zodiac called the "House of the Moon." The Planet Neptune has always been considered as associated with the Moon, and, as the part of the Zodiac I have mentioned is also called the First House of Water, the connection of Neptune whose very name is always associated with Water is then logical and easily understood.

Now, as the number of the Moon is always given as a 2, this explains why it is that the number 7 people have as their secondary number the 2, and get on well and make friends easily with all those born under the Moon numbers, namely, the 2nd, 11th, 20th, and 29th of any month, especially so if they are also born in the "House of the Moon," from the 21st of June to the end of July.

People born under the number 7, namely, on the 7th, 16th, or 25th of any month, are very independent, original, and have strongly marked individuality.

At heart they love change and travel, being restless in their natures. If they have the means of gratifying their desires they visit foreign countries and become keenly interested in the affairs of far-off lands. They devour books on travel and have a wide universal knowledge of the world at large.

They often make extremely good writers, painters, or poets, but in everything they do, they sooner or later show a peculiar philosophical outlook on life that tinges all their work.

As a class they care little about the material things of life; they often become rich by their original ideas or methods of business, but if they do they are just as likely to make large donations from their wealth to charities or institutions. The women of this number generally marry well, as they are always anxious about the future, and feel that they need some rock to rest on lest the waters of Fate sweep them away.

The number 7 people have good ideas about business, or rather their plans are good if they will only carry them out. They have usually a keen desire to travel and read a great deal about far-off countries. If they can they will become interested in matters concerning the sea, and in trade or business they often become merchants, exporters and importers, dealing with foreign countries, and owners or captains of ships if they can get the chance.

Number 7 people have very peculiar ideas about religion. They dislike to follow the beaten track; they create a religion of their own, but one that appeals to the imagination and based on the mysterious.

These people usually have remarkable dreams and a great leaning to occultism; they have the gift of intuition, clairvoyance, and a peculiar quieting magnetism of their own that has great influence over others.

Number 7 people should endeavour to carry out their plans and aims on all days that fall under their "own number," such as the 7th, 16th, or 25th of any month, but more especially when these dates fall in the "period of the 7," namely, from the 21st June to July 20th–27th—and less strongly from that date to the end of August.

The days of the week more fortunate or "lucky" for them are the same as for the number 2 people, namely, Sunday and Monday, especially if their "own number" falls on one of these days, or their interchangeable numbers of 1, 2, 4, such as the 1st, 2nd, 4th, 10th, 11th, 13th, 19th, 20th, 22nd, 28th, 29th, or 31st.

Their "lucky" colours are all shades of green, pale shades, also white and yellow, and they should avoid all heavy dark colours as much as possible.

Their "lucky" stones are moonstones, "cat's-eyes," and pearls, and if possible, they should wear a moonstone or a piece of moss agate next their skin.

CHEIRO'S BOOK OF NUMBERS

FAMOUS PEOPLE BORN UNDER THE NUMBER 7

Queen Elizabeth	Born 7th Sept.	Represents a 7
Louis XIV	,, 16th Sept.	,, ,, 7
Empress Charlotte of Mexico	,, 7th June	,, ,, 7
Lord Rosebery	,, 7th May	,, ,, 7
Lord Balfour	,, 25th July	,, ,, 7
Admiral Earl Beatty	,, 16th Jan.	,, ,, 7
Bonar Law, M.P.	,, 16th Sept.	,, ,, 7
Charles Dickens	,, 7th Feb.	,, ,, 7
Sir Joshua Reynolds	,, 16th July	,, ,, 7
Oscar Wilde	,, 16th Oct.	,, ,, 7
Ernst Haeckel (*Naturalist*)	,, 16th Feb.	,, ,, 7
Camille Flammarion (*Astronomer*)	,, 25th Feb.	,, ,, 7
Prince Imperial (Napoleon)	,, 16th Mar.	,, ,, 7
Sir John Franklin (*Explorer*)	,, 16th April	,, ,, 7
Robert Browning (*Poet*)	,, 7th May	,, ,, 7
Ralph Waldo Emerson (*Poet*)	,, 25th June	,, ,, 7
Dean Farrar	,, 7th Aug.	,, ,, 7
Bret Harte	,, 25th Aug.	,, ,, 7
Philip D. Armour (*founder of Armour & Co., Chicago*)	,, 16th May	,, ,, 7
Andrew Carnegie	,, 25th Nov.	,, ,, 7
Sir Isaac Newton (*Astronomer*)	,, 25th Dec.	,, ,, 7
Rousseau (*French Poet*)	,, 16th April	,, ,, 7
Sardou (*Author*)	,, 7th Sept.	,, ,, 7
De Witt Talmage (*Preacher*)	,, 7th Jan.	,, ,, 7
William Wordsworth (*Poet*)	,, 7th April	,, ,, 7

CHAPTER X

THE NUMBER 8

THE number 8 stands in symbolism for the Planet Saturn. This number influences all persons born on the 8th, 17th, or 26th in any month, but still more so if their birthday comes between the 21st December and the 26th January, which period is called the House of Saturn (Positive), and from the 26th January to February 19th–26th, the period called the House of Saturn (Negative).

These people are invariably much misunderstood in their lives, and perhaps for this reason they feel intensely lonely at heart.

They have deep and very intense natures, great strength of individuality; they generally play some important rôle on life's stage, but usually one which is fatalistic, or as the instrument of Fate for others.

If at all religious they go to extremes and are fanatics in their zeal. In any cause they take up, they attempt to carry it through in spite of all argument or opposition, and in doing so they generally make bitter and relentless enemies.

They often appear cold and undemonstrative, though in reality they have warm hearts towards the oppressed of all classes; but they hide their feelings and allow people to think just what they please.

These number 8 people are either great successes or great failures; there appears to be no happy medium in their case.

If ambitious, they generally aim for public life or government responsibility of some kind, and often hold very high positions involving great sacrifice on their part.

It is not, however, from a worldly standpoint, a fortunate number to be born under, and such persons often are called on to face the very greatest sorrows, losses, and humiliations.

The "lucky" colours for people born under the 8 are all shades of dark grey, black, dark blue, and purple. If number 8 persons were to dress in light colours they would look awkward, and as if there were something wrong with them.

The number 8 being a Saturn number, Saturday is therefore their most important day, but on account of the number 4 having influence on a Sunday and in a secondary way on a Monday, the number 8 people will find Saturday, Sunday, and Monday their most important days.

Number 8 people should endeavour to carry out their plans and aims on all days that fall under their "own number," such as the 8th, 17th, or 26th in any month, but more especially so when these dates fall in the "period of the 8," namely, from the 21st December to January 20th–27th, and from that date to February 19th–26th; also if these dates fall on a Saturday, Sunday, or Monday, or their interchangeable number, which is 4, such as the 4th, 13th, 22nd, or 31st.

Their "lucky" stones are the amethyst and the darktoned sapphire, also the black pearl or the black diamond and if possible they should wear one of these next their skin.

The number 8 is a difficult number to explain. It represents two worlds, the material and the spiritual. It is in fact, if one regards it, like two circles just touching together.

It is composed of two equal numbers: 4 and 4.

From the earliest ages it has been associated with the symbol of an irrevocable Fate, both in connection with the lives of individuals or nations. In Astrology it stands for Saturn, which is also called the Planet of Fate.

One side of the nature of this number represents upheaval, revolution, anarchy, waywardness and eccentricities of all kinds.

The other side represents philosophic thought, a strong leaning towards occult studies, religious devotion, concentration of purpose, zeal for any cause espoused, and a fatalistic outlook colouring all actions.

All persons who have the number 8 clearly associated with their lives feel that they are distinct and different from their fellows. At heart they are lonely; they are misunderstood, and they seldom reap the reward for the good they may do while they are living. After their death they are often extolled, their works praised, and lasting tributes offered to their memory.

Those on the lower plane generally come into conflict with human justice and have some tragic ending to their lives. Those on the higher plane carry their misunderstood motives and lay bare the tragedy of their souls before Divine Justice.

To distinguish in which of these two classes a number 8 person falls, one must find by the comparison of their "fadic" numbers if they are completely dominated by the recurrence of 8 in the principal events of their lives, or if some other equally powerful number such as the 1, 3 or 6 series does not more or less balance the sequel of events registered under the 8 and all its series.

If the latter is the case, one may be sure that by the long series of reincarnations they have passed through, they have paid the price in some former state, and are now passing towards the higher, where Divine Justice will give them their reward.

If, on the contrary, we find that the person is completely dominated by the number 8, always recurring in important events, or if instead of 8 the nearly equally fatalistic number of 4 is continually recurring, we may then be sure that we are in the presence of one of those strange playthings of Fate with the possibilities that tragedy may be interwoven in their Destiny.

In the more ordinary tragedies of everyday life, we can find an illuminating example in the life and execution of Crippen, whose principal actions were singularly influenced by the terrible combination of the 8 and the 4.

Looking back over his career, and especially the events which led up to his paying that terrible forfeit at the hands of the law, one will find these numbers associated in the most dramatic way with this man's life, as illustrated by the following facts:

The figures of the year he was born in (1862), if added

together, produce an 8 (17 equals 1 plus 7 equals 8). He was born on the 26th of January, or 2 plus 6 equals 8.

His wife was not seen alive after dinner with him on the 31st January, which is a 4, and the month of January is itself called the House of Saturn, whose number is an 8.

He made his statement to Inspector Drew (which was later to be used as overwhelming evidence against him) on the 8th July.

The human remains were found in the cellar on 13th July, which again makes the number 4.

To try to escape he chose the name "Robinson," which has, strange to say, 8 letters in it.

He was recognised on board the *Montrose* on the 22nd July, which again equals a 4.

The name of the ship he chose to leave Europe by (the *Montrose*) has 8 letters, and the ship that brought him back to his doom, the *Megantic*, was also composed of 8 letters.

He was arrested, as this ship reached Canada, on the morning of the 31st July, which again equals 4.

His trial finished on Saturday, 22nd October, which is again the 4, and October being the month of "the detriment of Saturn" gives again the 8.

The occult number by which Saturday is designated is an 8.

His execution was fixed for the 8th November.

His appeal was heard and refused on Saturday, 5th November. The 5 added to the 8, which Saturday is a symbol of, again makes the figure 13, which number again equals a 4.

When his appeal failed, the date of execution was changed to the 23rd November. The addition of 2-3 makes a 5, and the division of the Zodiac which represents this portion of November is designated as a 3; and this 3, if added to the date (the 23rd), makes the figure 26, which by addition (2 plus 6) again equals 8. Or if the 3 were added to the number of 23 we would get 26 or the 8.

The symbol of the number 8, I may also mention, from time immemorial, in occult studies, is called the "symbol of human justice."

Lastly, *when Crippen's "Key numbers", the 4 and 8, came together, it was the fatal year of his life.* He was 48 *years old when executed.*

It is not my province to judge or condemn this unfortunate being. Crippen, in any case, suffered as few men have been called upon to suffer; but I may add that the combination of such numbers as 4 and 8 as the "Key numbers" in any life, indicate an individual terribly under the influence of Fate, and one especially unfortunate through his or her affections.

I have followed out many cases of people having similar "Key numbers," and in every case they seem sooner or later to come into conflict with what the 8 represents, namely, the symbol of "human justice." They are generally condemned, even in ordinary social life, by the weight of circumstantial evidence, and they usually die with their secret, appealing, as it were, from the sentence of "human justice," which, as a rule, has been against them, to that of the Divine Justice in the world beyond.

The occult symbol of 8 has from time immemorial been represented by the figure of Justice with a Sword pointing upwards and a Balance or Scales in the left hand.

There are many very curious things in history as regards this number. The Greeks called it the number of Justice on account of its equal divisions of equally even numbers.

The Jews practised circumcision on the 8th day after birth. At their Feast of Dedication they kept 8 candles burning, and this Feast lasted 8 days.

Eight prophets were descended from Rahab.

There were 8 sects of Pharisees.

Noah was the 8th in direct descent from Adam.

The strange number of three eights (888) is considered by students of Occultism to be the number of Jesus Christ in His aspect as the Redeemer of the world. Curiously enough, the addition of 888 makes 24 and 2 plus 4 gives the 6 which is the number of Venus, the representative of Love.

This number 888 given to Christ is in direct opposition to 666 which Revelation says "is the number of the Beast or the number of Man." The numbers 666 if added together gives 18 (1 plus 8 equals 9). This 9 is the number of Mars, the symbol of War, destruction, and force, which is decidedly the opposition of the 6 with the symbol of Love.

REMARKABLE PEOPLE BORN UNDER THE 8

Mary I of England (called Bloody Queen Mary)	Born 17th Feb.	Represents an 8
King Albert of Belgium	„ 8th April	„ „ 8
Queen Mary	„ 26th May	„ „ 8
Alfonso XIII of Spain	„ 17th May	„ „ 8
Joseph Chamberlain	„ 8th July	„ „ 8
George Bernard Shaw	„ 26th July	„ „ 8
David Lloyd George	„ 17th Jan.	„ „ 8
Prince Albert (Consort of Queen Victoria)	„ 26th Aug.	„ „ 8
Admiral Dewey (U.S.A.)	„ 26th Dec.	„ „ 8
Bernadotte, King of Sweden	„ 26th Jan.	„ „ 8
Colonel Cody (Buffalo Bill)	„ 26th Feb.	„ „ 8
Wilkie Collins (*Author*)	„ 8th Jan.	„ „ 8
Louis Condé of France	„ 8th Sept.	„ „ 8
Sir Humphrey Davy	„ 17th Dec.	„ „ 8
Gounod (*Composer*)	„ 17th June	„ „ 8
Jenner (*Discoverer of Vaccines*)	„ 17th May	„ „ 8
La Fontaine	„ 8th July	„ „ 8
Mary, Queen of Scots	„ 8th Dec.	„ „ 8
Sir John Millais (*Painter*)	„ 8th June	„ „ 8
General von Moltke	„ 26th Oct.	„ „ 8
Pierpont-Morgan (*Financier*)	„ 17th April	„ „ 8
Richard I (Cœur de Lion)	„ 8th Sept.	„ „ 8
J. D. Rockefeller (*Oil Magnate*)	„ 8th July	„ 8
Jules Verne (*Novelist*)	„ 8th Feb.	„ „ 8
John Wesley (*Preacher*)	„ 17th June	„ „ 8

CHAPTER XI

THE NUMBER 9

THE number 9 stands in symbolism for the Planet Mars. This number influences all persons born on the 9th, 18th, and 27th of any month, but still more so if their birthday falls in the period between the 21st March and April 19th–26th (called the House of Mars Positive) or in the period between the 21st October and November 20th–27th (called the House of Mars Negative).

Number 9 persons are fighters in all they attempt in life. They usually have difficult times in their early years, but generally they are, in the end, successful by their grit, strong will, and determination.

In character, they are hasty in temper, impulsive, independent, and desire to be their own masters.

When the number 9 is noticed to be more than usually dominant in the dates and events of their lives they will be found to make great enemies, to cause strife and opposition wherever they may be, and they are often wounded or killed either in warfare or in the battle of life.

They have great courage and make excellent soldiers or leaders in any cause they espouse.

Their greatest dangers arise from foolhardiness and impulsiveness in word and action. They are also peculiarly prone to accidents from fire and explosions and rarely get through life without injury from such causes. As a general rule they go under many operations by the surgeon's knife.

They usually experience many quarrels and strife in their home life, either with their own relations or with the family they marry into.

They strongly resent criticism, and even when not conceited, they have always a good opinion of themselves, brooking no interference with their plans. They like to be "looked up to" and recognised as "the head of the house."

They are resourceful and excellent in organisation, but they must have the fullest control; if not, they lose heart and stand aside and let things go to pieces.

For affection and sympathy they will do almost anything, and the men of this number can be made the greatest fools of, if some clever woman gets pulling at their heartstrings.

As a rule they get on with persons whose birth date is one of the series of 3, 6, or 9, such as those born on the 3rd, 6th, 9th, 12th, 15th, 18th, 21st, 24th, 27th, or 30th of any month. All these numbers are in harmonious vibration to the number 9 people.

This number 9 has some very curious properties. It is the only number in calculation that, multiplied by any number, always reproduces itself, as for example 9 times 2 is 18, and 8 plus 1 becomes again the 9, and so on *with every number it is multiplied by*.

It is, perhaps, not uninteresting to notice that:

At the 9th day the ancients buried their dead.

At the 9th hour the Saviour died on the Cross.

The Romans held a feast in memory of their dead every 9th year.

In some of the Hebrew writings it is taught that God has 9 times descended to this earth:

1st in the Garden of Eden,
2nd at the confusion of tongues at Babel,
3rd at the destruction of Sodom and Gomorrah,
4th to Moses at Horeb,
5th at Sinai when the Ten Commandments were given,
6th to Balaam,
7th to Elisha,
8th in the Tabernacle,
9th in the Temple at Jerusalem,
and it is taught that at the 10th coming this earth will pass away and a new one will be created.

Both the First and Second Temples of the Jews were destroyed on the 9th day of the Jewish month called Ab. On the 9th day of Ab Jews who follow their religion cannot wear the Talith and Phylacteries until the Sun has set.

There are so many curious things connected with the number 9 that it would not be possible to deal with one-half of them in a book of this description.

This number is supposed to be a fortunate one to be born under, provided one controls it and is not carried away by the excesses of temper and violence that it also represents.

The "lucky" colours for persons born under the number 9 are all shades of crimson or red, also all rose tones and pink.

Their most important days in the week are Tuesday, Thursday, and Friday, but more especially Tuesday (called Mars Day).

Number 9 people should endeavour to carry out their plans and aims on all days that fall under their "own number," such as the 9th, 18th, or 27th in any month, but more especially when these dates fall in the "period of the 9," between the 21st March and April 19th–26th, or from the 21st October to November 20th–27th. And when the 9th, 18th, or 27th falls on their "own day," as mentioned above, or one of their interchangeable numbers which are the 3 and 6, such as the 3rd, 6th, 12th, 15th, 21st, 24th, and 30th.

Their "lucky" stones are the ruby, garnet, and bloodstone, and they should wear one of these stones next their skin.

For all purposes of occult calculation the numbers 7 and 9 are considered the most important of all.

The 7 has always been understood to relate to the spiritual plane, acting as the God or creative force on the Earth, and being creative, it is the uplifting "urge" towards the higher development of the spiritual in humanity.

The 9 on the contrary, being, in the Planetary World, the representative of the Planet Mars, is the number of physical force in every form, and consequently stands in relation to the material.

When this explanation is carefully considered it throws an illuminating light on that mysterious text in Revelation, chapter xiii. verse 18: "Here is wisdom. Let him that hath understanding count the number of the beast, for it is the number of man, and his number is 666."

This strange text has puzzled the theological mind for centuries, yet if you will take the trouble to add 666 together you will get 18, and 1 plus 8 gives you the figure 9, which in turn represents the 9 Planets of our Solar System, the 9 numbers upon which man builds all his calculations, and beyond which he cannot go except by continual repetition of the numbers 1 to 9.

"6 6 6" producing its "spirit number" (as explained in the preceding page) of 9 is therefore, in all truth as Revelation states, "the number of man."

The hidden meaning of this number is one of the greatest secrets of occultism, and has been concealed in a thousand ways, just as the cryptic text in Revelation has hidden it for centuries from the minds of Theologians.

The number 9 representing man and everything to do with the physical and material plane, is the number of force, energy, destruction and war in its most dominant quality. In its relation to ordinary life it denotes energy, ambition, leadership, dominion. It represents iron, the metal from which the weapons of warfare are made, and the Planet Mars which it stands for in Astrology is the Ruler of the Zodiacal Sign Aries which is the Sign of the Zodiac which governs England. This symbolism was evidently well known by Shakespeare when he wrote, "England, thou seat of Mars."

The number 9 is an emblem of matter that can never be destroyed, so the number 9 when multiplied by any number always reproduces itself, no matter what the extent of the number is that has been employed.

The Novendiale was a fast in the Roman Catholic Church to avert calamities, and from this came the Roman Catholic system of Neuvaines.

In Freemasonry there is an Order of "Nine Elected Knights," and in the working of this Order 9 roses, 9 lights and 9 knocks must be used.

All ancient races encouraged a fear of the number 9, and all its multiples.

The number 9 is considered a fortunate number to be born under, provided the man or woman does not ask for a peaceful or monotonous life, and can control their nature in not making enemies.

The following are a few illustrations of such birthdays:

Kaiser Wilhelm	Born 27th Jan.	Represents a 9
King Edward VII	,, 9th Nov.	,, ,, 9
Sir Evelyn Wood, V.C.	,, 9th Feb.	,, ,, 9
President Theodore Roosevelt (U.S.A.)	,, 27th Oct.	,, ,, 9
President Grover Cleveland (U.S.A.)	,, 18th Mar.	,, ,, 9
Lord Carson (*Irish Leader*)	,, 9th Feb.	,, ,, 9
Sam Gompers (*Labour Leader, U.S.A.*)	,, 27th Jan.	,, ,, 9
Ernest Renan (*Author*)	,, 27th Feb.	,, ,, 9
President Ulysses Grant	,, 27th April	,, ,, 9
Sir James Barrie (*Author*)	,, 9th May	,, ,, 9
Julia Ward Howe (*of Battle-Hymn fame*)	,, 27th May	,, ,, 9
Jay Gould (*Financier*)	,, 27th May	,, ,, 9
Elizabeth, Empress of Austria	,, 18th Aug.	,, ,, 9
Franz Josef, Emperor of Austria	,, 18th Aug.	,, ,, 9
Frederick III of Germany	,, 18th Oct.	,, ,, 9
Kepler (*Astronomer*)	,, 27th Dec.	,, ,, 9
Louis Kossuth (*Hungarian Patriot*)	,, 27th April	,, ,, 9
Leopold II, of Belgium	,, 9th April	,, ,, 9
Nicholas II, of Russia	,, 18th May	,, ,, 9
Paganini (*Violinist*)	,, 18th Feb.	,, ,, 9
Whitelaw Reid (*Statesman*)	,, 27th Oct.	,, ,, 9
George Stephenson (*Inventor of Steam Engine*)	,, 9th June	,, ,, 9

CHAPTER XII

THE OCCULT SYMBOLISM OF "COMPOUND" NUMBERS, WITH ILLUSTRATIONS

I AM now going to put before my readers one of the most amazing systems comprised in the occult calculations of names and numbers that it has been my good fortune to elucidate. This system, which has never before been made public on the lines I am going to present it, will, I know, be of inestimable value to those who may care to follow the rules I shall give.

I feel sure, from long experience, that the occult philosophy I am now about to pass on will be of the greatest *practical utility* to every man or woman, who wishes for aid in the hard struggle for existence that is, alas, the fate of so many sons and daughters of humanity.

Shakespeare, that Prince of Philosophers, whose thoughts will adorn English literature for all time, laid down the well-known axiom: "There is a tide in the affairs of men which, taken at the flood, leads on to fortune." The question has been asked again and again: Is there some means of knowing when the moment has come *to take the tide at the flood*?

My answer to this question is, that the Great Architect of the Universe in His Infinite Wisdom so created all things in such harmony of design that He endowed the human mind with some part of that omnipotent knowledge which is the attribute of the Divine Mind as the Creator of all.

It is this desire for knowledge implanted in the mind of humanity that places mankind above the animal creation, and makes men and women as "gods" in their desire "to know."

We are told that Solomon the King asked to be given Wisdom as the greatest gift that God could give him, and in the ancient Hebrew of the Book of Solomon we can yet read his inspiring words:

> I thank Thee, O Great Creator of the Universe, that Thou hast taught me the secrets of the Planets, that I mayst know the Times and Seasons of Things, the secrets of men's hearts, their thoughts, and the nature of their being. Thou gavest unto me this knowledge which is the foundation of all my Wisdom.

It is these self-same "Secrets of the Planets" that I have endeavoured to teach in these pages.

I now ask my readers to give their attention and concentration to the following system which I will put as briefly and in as clear language as possible.

To find the exact day in any month of the year whose vibration will be favourable, or in other words "lucky" to any individual, the simplest rule is to work out by the following table the occult number produced by the letters of their name.

This ancient Chaldean and Hebrew alphabet sets out the number or value of each letter. It is the best system I know for this purpose; its origin is lost in antiquity, but it is believed that it was originated by the Chaldeans, who were masters in all magical arts, and by them passed to the Hebrews.

A	=	1	N	=	5
B	=	2	O	=	7
C	=	3	P	=	8
D	=	4	Q	=	1
E	=	5	R	=	2
F	=	8	S	=	3
G	=	3	T	=	4
H	=	5	U	=	6
I or J	=	1	V	=	6
K	=	2	W	=	6
L	=	3	X	=	5
M	=	4	Y	=	1
			Z	=	7

It will be seen that there is no number 9 given in the above alphabet, for the simple reason that those ancient masters of Occultism knew that in the "Highest Sphere" the number 9 represents the 9-lettered name of God, and for this reason no single letter was ascribed to it.

If, however, the letters in a name should total up and produce the number 9, the meaning of it is that given as I set out in the previous chapter dealing with the number 9, and for the compound numbers of the 9 such as the 18, 27, etc.

The next important question to answer is the following: Are all the Christian and Surnames to be added together to find the last digit or number?

The answer to that is, that it is *the most used* Christian and Surname that must be added together to give the Key number; when the Surname is more used or more in evidence than the Christian name, then it is taken to give the Key number.

I have only space in a book of this description to give illustrations of a few well-known names. One I will take was always spoken of as Lloyd George—the other, Ex-Prime Minister, was called simply Baldwin.

The names Lloyd George and the Ex-Prime Minister of England, if transcribed into numbers are as follows:

```
L = 3                G = 3
L = 3                E = 5
O = 7                O = 7
Y = 1                R = 2
D = 4                G = 3
    —                E = 5
   18 = 9               —
                       25 = 7

B = 2
A = 1
L = 3
D = 4
W = 6
I = 1
N = 5
    —
   22 = 4
```

In Lloyd George's case, the word Lloyd alone produces the single number of 9, which, as I have previously explained, is connected with persons who have a hard fight with circumstances in their early lives and who, if they rise to positions of authority in nations, are often the cause of wars or (as with Lloyd George) play an active part in them.

The word George in itself produces the single number of 7. This is, as I have also previously explained, a magnetic number, and favourable if used by itself. In this case, however, the two names are never used alone, but always together, as Lloyd George: now add the two single numbers of each name together—7 plus 9 and you get *the compound number of* 16, the occult symbolism of which is "a Shattered Citadel" or "a Lightning-struck Tower." A full description of the compound numbers will be found later in these pages.

If, however, the word David were added it would produce another 7, and if the name David Lloyd George was employed *in continuous use* instead of Lloyd George, the addition of the 7 for the word David would make the total of the three names the number 23, which, as will be seen in Chapter XIII dealing with the meaning of the compound numbers, is considered a fortunate number.

However, by some hidden law of destiny over which man has no control, he became known and called Lloyd George, and so this name foreshadowed that he would one day in his marvellous career fulfil the symbolism of "a Shattered Citadel" or "a Lightning-struck Tower."

The other Ex-Prime Minister was for some unknown reason never called by his political followers or the general public anything else but Baldwin. This name, as you will notice, totals up to the number 22, and in its single figure to a 4.

The number 4, as I explained in a previous chapter, is not considered a fortunate number; people under it are usually misunderstood. They work hard and strive earnestly to carry out their ideas, but their plans are difficult and usually meet with great opposition.

Taking again these two well-known public leaders for another illustration, I now come to the most curious side

CHEIRO'S BOOK OF NUMBERS

of this study of numerology, namely, that the "compound" numbers have *an extraordinary meaning of their own*, which throws an added light on the mysterious connection they have in the still deeper side of occultism as applied to people's names.

Taking again the name Lloyd George, we find the first word Lloyd gives the "compound" number 18. In occult symbolism this number is represented as "a rayed moon from which blood is dropping like rain; in a field below a wolf and a dog are catching drops of blood in their opened mouths."

Taking the word George, the "compound" number is 25. In symbolism this number is classed as "a number of strength gained by experience and ultimate gain through strife."

The conclusion therefore is that if Lloyd George had become known in the world as plain George he would have retained to the end the high position he had gained.

Lloyd George was born on January 17th; he was therefor by his birth a number 8 man, which is unfortunately not in harmonious vibration with his name number, and further, by being an 8, increases the fatalistic indications given by the number of his name—a 16.

The "compound" number of 22, made by the name Baldwin, in the same occult symbolism of numbers is not at all favourable from a purely worldly sense as a leader of men. The single number of a name, it must be remembered, represents the man or woman *as they appear to be*. The "double" or "compound" number represents *the hidden forces that use the man or woman as their instrument.* The symbolism of the number 22 is "a good man blinded by the folly of others, with a knapsack on his back full of Errors; he offers no defence against a ferocious tiger who is biting him."

I have, of course, no political leanings in any direction; I merely as your mentor in these studies

Sketch your world exactly as it goes—without offence—
to friends or foes.

and have only quoted the symbolism given to these numbers since the most ancient times.

SIR AUSTEN CHAMBERLAIN

As Sir Austen Chamberlain was generally spoken of as Austen Chamberlain, his numbers are as follows:

```
A = 1              C = 3
U = 6              H = 5
S = 3              A = 1
T = 4              M = 4
E = 5              B = 2
N = 5              E = 5
   ––              R = 2
   24 = 6          L = 3
                   A = 1
                   I = 1
                   N = 5
                      ––
                      32 = 5
```

Both the single numbers and the compound numbers in this name are singularly fortunate, especially if used separately, as I have explained in a previous chapter; the number 6 is usually found associated with persons who rise to high positions of authority—especially in political life.

The compound number 24 is also favourable, and in occult symbolism it is put down as a number that brings "the assistance and association of people of high rank, and gain through such association."

The simple number of 5, as in the name Chamberlain, is, as I said on a previous page, a "lucky" number, especially for those who lead changeable lives with a large element of risk, change, and speculation involved in their career; while the compound number of 32 is also given in occult symbolism as a magical number and is put down as associated with what is called "the Paths of Wisdom."

His title of "Sir" produces the number 6, again a favourable number, and if we now add the single numbers of all the three together, we get 6 plus 6 plus 5 equals 17, a compound number whose occult symbolism is curiously enough the 8-pointed Star of Venus, a symbol of Peace and Love, which is peculiarly suitable for the career of a man who made superhuman efforts towards bringing peace between nations at Locarno. If, however, he was only known as Austen Chamberlain, the total of these two words produce the number 11, which, as my readers will see farther on, gives warning of "hidden dangers, trial and treachery from others."

Sir Austen Chamberlain was born on October 16th. Neither the single number of 7 nor the compound are in harmonious vibration with the number of his name. This was not a favourable promise for a successful ending of his career, as is explained later on in these pages.

RAMSAY MACDONALD

We will take the first Labour Prime Minister of England for our next illustration. His numbers are as follows:

```
R = 2            M = 4
A = 1            A = 1
M = 4            C = 3
S = 3            D = 4
A = 1            O = 7
Y = 1            N = 5
    —            A = 1
   12 = 3        L = 3
                 D = 4
                    —
                   32 = 5
```

It will be seen that the name Ramsay produces 3 as its simple number and 12 for its compound number.

As I have explained earlier in this book, the single number denotes the person *as he appears to be* in the eyes of his fellow mortals, while the compound number represents the hidden forces in the background of the career.

In this case, the single number 3 is strong and powerful, and is generally associated with ambitious people who gain positions of authority and who do especially well in government departments.

The occult symbolism of the compound number 12 is, however, that of "the Victim or the Sacrifice."

The letters of the name MacDonald produce the single number of 5, an excellent number, as I explained before, and the compound number 32 is, as in the case of Sir Austen Chamberlain, also a good number with its symbolism of "the Paths of Wisdom."

The addition, however, of the two single numbers of the name Ramsay MacDonald, 5 plus 3, produces an 8, a number which, I have explained earlier, represents two worlds, the material and the spiritual, one side associated with philosophic thought, concentration of purpose and zeal for any cause espoused, the other representing upheavals and revolutions.

This combination, taken with the meaning of the compound number that stands for his Christian name giving the symbolism of "the Victim or the Sacrifice," foreshadowed very clearly that Ramsay MacDonald, no matter what his great qualities, would in the end be made "the victim" or "the sacrifice" of his political party and be associated in his career with upheavals and revolutions.

The addition of the numbers of the two names 12 and 32 produces the compound number of 44, which in the explanation of compound numbers given in Chapter XIII reads: "This number is full of the gravest warnings for the future. It foreshadows disasters brought about by association with others." A decidedly ominous indication of the future of the leader of one of England's political parties. Further, as he was born on October 12th, the single number of which is a 3, this is not in harmonious vibration with his Name number, an 8. Consequently one might have expected a great deal of muddle and jumble to be associated with his career.

If this man had really understood the extraordinary meaning there is in a name when transcribed into numbers, he would never have allowed his party or his public to call him by the single word Ramsay. He should never have allowed such familiarity, but insisted on being called, *if he could do it*, by the single word MacDonald with its magical number of 32.

Later on in this book (Chapter XXXI) will be found examples from the names of Presidents of the United States such as George Washington, Abraham Lincoln, Grover Cleveland, Warren G. Harding, Theodore Roosevelt, Woodrow Wilson, Calvin Coolidge, and Herbert Hoover.

* * * * *

In the following chapter I will explain the symbolism that from the most ancient times has been given to what is called "compound numbers," and at the same time I will give the system I have alluded to at the beginning of this chapter, whereby readers will be able to understand how it is that they can know when the "lucky" day comes, so that they may be able to take hold of any good opportunity which may present itself.

CHAPTER XIII

THE "COMPOUND" OR "SPIRITUAL" NUMBERS FULLY DESCRIBED

IN the preceding chapters I have given the meanings of what are called the principal or "single" numbers—also called the "root" numbers—from 1 to 9. I will now proceed with the next step in this curious study of Numerology, namely, the explanation of the occult symbolism given to what are called the "double" or "compound" numbers, and how such knowledge may be made use of in everyday life.

Although this is a much more advanced and more difficult part of the study of numbers, I will endeavour to make it as clear and as easy to understand as I have endeavoured to do with the single numbers in the earlier chapters.

Before launching out into this side of the subject, I must, I feel, give a few words of explanation so as to prepare my readers for what is to follow.

I have already explained that the single numbers denote what the man or woman *appears to be* in the eyes of their fellow mortals, while the double or compound numbers show the hidden influences that play their rôle behind the scenes as it were, and in some mysterious way often foreshadow the future or the hidden current of destiny of the individual.

When one passes the major or root numbers of 1 to 9, what is called the greater symbolism of numbers commences, and continues until 5 times 9 is reached, or the number 45; at this point the mystical number of 7 is brought into operation and added to the number of 45, producing 52, which stands for the 52 weeks of a year. This number of 52, multiplied by 7, gives 364 as the ordinary days of the year in that ancient period of Time when trade unionism had not made its appearance. These ancient and wonderful people, however, used the 365th day of each year as *the one great festival holiday of all*, and *no work of any kind* was allowed to be done by man, woman, child, or beast. This number of 365 is based on the passage of the Sun through the twelve divisions of the Zodiac, which is the origin of the calculation of the year period which is found in every civilisation.

As I said before, the meaning of the single numbers from 1 to 9 represents how the man or woman appears in the eyes of his fellows. They are the numbers of *individuality and personality*.

All numbers from 10 up become in symbolism "double" or "compound" numbers; the 12, if we take it for an example, has for its root or fadic number a single number such as the 3, but at the same time the 1 and 2 of which the twelve is composed are "compound" and have a meaning of their own distinct from the number 3.

How and in what age these "compound" numbers became illustrated by symbolism, we do not know and never can know. We can only say that they appear to have always existed.

Symbols may be called the Language of Nature, and as such we must take them.

The meanings ascribed to the numbers 1 to 9 belong then to *the physical or material side of things*, and "compound" numbers from 10 on belong to the more *occult or spiritual side of life*. Distinct symbolism has been given to the "compound" numbers up to that mysterious number of 52, and this symbolism I will now proceed to give in as clear language as it may be possible to translate them. I have already illustrated in a previous chapter by examples from names such as Lloyd George, Baldwin, Austen Chamberlain, and Ramsay MacDonald, the information one is able to get by knowing the meaning of the "compound" number and using it in relation to the information given by the single number, but later on it will be my privilege to explain a still more practical application of this knowledge which will enable one actually to pick out what days will be fortunate and what will be unfortunate, which will be, I think, of inestimable value to my readers.

The universally accepted symbolism of the compound numbers in ancient times was given in pictures and may still be found in the Tarot Cards which have been handed down to us from the most distant ages and whose origin is lost in antiquity.

10. Symbolised as the "Wheel of Fortune." It is a number of honour, of faith and self-confidence, of rise and fall; one's name will be known for good or evil, according to one's desires; it is a fortunate number in the sense that one's plans are likely to be carried out.
11. This is an ominous number to occultists. It gives warning of hidden dangers, trial, and treachery from others. It has a symbol of "a Clenched Hand," and "a Lion Muzzled," and of a person who will have great difficulties to contend against.
12. The symbolism of this number is suffering and anxiety of mind. It is also indicated as "the Sacrifice" or "the Victim" and generally foreshadows one being sacrificed for the plans or intrigues of others.
13. This is a number indicating change of plans, place, and such-like, and is not unfortunate, as is generally supposed. In some of the ancient writings it is said, "He who understands the number 13 will be given power and dominion." It is symbolised by the picture of "a Skeleton" or "Death," with a scythe reaping down men, in a field of new-grown grass where young faces and heads appear cropping up on every side. It is a number of upheaval and destruction. It is a symbol of "Power" which if wrongly used will wreak destruction upon itself. It is a number of warning of the unknown or unexpected, if it becomes a "compound" number in one's calculations.
14. This is a number of movement, combination of people and things, and danger from natural forces, such as tempests, water, air, or fire. This number is fortunate for dealings with money, speculation, and changes in business, but there is always a strong element of risk and danger attached to it, but generally owing to the actions and foolhardiness of others. If this number comes out in calculations of future events the person should be warned to act with caution and prudence.
15. This is a number of occult significance, of magic and mystery; but as a rule it does not represent the higher side of occul-

tism, its meaning being that the persons represented by it will use every art of magic they can to carry out their purpose. If associated with a good or fortunate single number, it can be very lucky and powerful, but if associated with one of the peculiar numbers, such as a 4 or an 8, the person it represents will not scruple to use any sort of art, or even "black magic," to gain what he or she desires.

It is peculiarly associated with "good talkers," often with eloquence, gifts of Music and Art and a dramatic personality, combined with a certain voluptuous temperament and strong personal magnetism. For obtaining money, gifts, and favours from others it is a fortunate number.

16. This number has a most peculiar occult symbolism. It is pictured by "a Tower Struck by Lightning from which a man is falling with a Crown on his head." It is also called "the Shattered Citadel."

    It gives warning of some strange fatality awaiting one, also danger of accidents and defeat of one's plans. If it appears as a "compound" number relating to the future, it is a warning sign that should be carefully noted and plans made in advance in the endeavour to avert its fatalistic tendency.

17. This is a highly spiritual number, and is expressed in symbolism by the 8-pointed Star of Venus: a symbol of "Peace and Love." It is also called "the Star of the Magi" and expresses that the person it represents has risen superior in spirit to the trials and difficulties of his life or his career. It is considered a "number of immortality" and that the person's name "lives after him." It is a fortunate number if it works out in relation to future events, provided it is not associated with the single numbers of fours and eights.

18. This number has a difficult symbolism to translate. It is pictured as "a rayed moon from which drops of blood are falling; a wolf and a hungry dog are seen below catching the falling drops of blood in their opened mouths, while still lower a crab is seen hastening to join then." It is symbolic of materialism striving to destroy the spiritual side of the nature. It generally associates a person with bitter quarrels, even family ones, also with war, social upheavals, revolutions; and in some cases it indicates making money and position through wars or by wars. It is, however, a warning of treachery, deception by others, also danger from the elements, such as storms, danger from water, fires and

explosions. When this "compound" number appears in working out dates in advance, such a date should be taken with a great amount of care, caution, and circumspection.

19. This number is regarded as fortunate and extremely favourable. It is symbolised as "the Sun" and is called "the Prince of Heaven." It is a number promising happiness, success, esteem and honour, and promises success in one's plans for the future.

20. This number is called "the Awakening"; also "the Judgment." It is symbolised by the figure of a winged angel sounding a trumpet, while from below a man, a woman, and a child are seen rising from a tomb with their hands clasped in prayer.

   This number has a peculiar interpretation: the awakening of new purpose, new plans, new ambitions, the call to action, but for some great purpose, cause or duty. It is not a material number and consequently is a doubtful one as far as worldly success is concerned.

   If used in relation to a future event, it denotes delays, hindrances to one's plans, which can only be conquered through the development of the spiritual side of the nature.

21. This number is symbolised by the picture of "the Universe," and it is also called "the Crown of the Magi." It is a number of advancement, honours, elevation in life, and general success. It means victory after a long fight, for "the Crown of the Magi" is only gained after long initiation and tests of determination. It is a fortunate number of promise if it appears in any connection with future events.

22. This number is symbolised by "a Good Man blinded by the folly of others, with a knapsack on his back full of Errors." In this picture he appears to offer no defence against a ferocious tiger which is attacking him. It is a warning number of illusion and delusion, a good person who lives in a fool's paradise; a dreamer of dreams who awakens only when surrounded by danger. It is also a number of false judgment owing to the influence of others.

   As a number in connection with future events its warning and meaning should be carefully noted.

23. This number is called "the Royal Star of the Lion." It is a promise of success, help from superiors and protection from those in high places. In dealing with future events it is a most fortunate number and a promise of success for one's plans.

24. This number is also fortunate; it promises the assistance and association of those of rank and position with one's plans; it also denotes gain through love and the opposite sex; it is a favourable number when it comes out in relation to future events.
25. This is a number denoting strength gained through experience, and benefits obtained through observation of people and things. It is not deemed exactly "lucky," as its success is given through strife and trials in the earlier life. It is favourable when it appears in regard to the future.
26. This number is full of the gravest warnings for the future. It foreshadows disasters brought about by association with others; ruin, by bad speculations, by partnerships, unions, and bad advice.

    If it comes out in connection with future events one should carefully consider the path one is treading.
27. This is a good number and is symbolised as "the Sceptre." It is a promise of authority, power, and command. It indicates that reward will come from the productive intellect; that the creative faculties have sown good seeds that will reap a harvest. Persons with this "compound" number at their back should carry out their own ideas and plans. It is a fortunate number if it appears in any connection with future events.
28. This number is full of contradictions. It indicates a person of great promise and possibilities who is likely to see all taken away from him unless he carefully provides for the future. It indicates loss through trust in others, opposition and competition in trade, danger of loss through law, and the likelihood of having to begin life's road over and over again.

    It is not a fortunate number for the indication of future events.
29. This number indicates uncertainties, treachery, and deception of others; it foreshadows trials, tribulation, and unexpected dangers, unreliable friends, and grief and deception caused by members of the opposite sex. It gives grave warning if it comes out in anything concerning future events.
30. This is a number of thoughtful deduction, retrospection, and mental superiority over one's fellows, but, as it seems to belong completely to the mental plane, the persons it represents are likely to put all material things on one side —not because they have to, but because they wish to do so

For this reason it is neither fortunate nor unfortunate, for either depends on the mental outlook of the person it represents. It can be all powerful, but it is just as often indifferent according to the will or desire of the person.

31. This number is very similar to the preceding one, except that the person it represents is even more self-contained, lonely, and isolated from his fellows. It is not a fortunate number from a worldly or material standpoint.

32. This number has a magical power like the single 5, or the "compound" numbers 14 and 23. It is usually associated with combinations of people or nations. It is a fortunate number if the person it represents holds to his own judgment and opinions; if not, his plans are likely to become wrecked by the stubbornness and stupidity of others. It is a favourable number if it appears in connection with future events.

33. This number has no potency of its own, and consequently has the same meaning as the 24—which is also a 6—and the next to it in its own series of "compound" numbers.

34. Has the same meaning as the number 25, which is the next to it in its own series of "compound" numbers.

35. Has the same meaning as the number 26, which is the next to it in its own series of "compound" numbers.

36. Has the same meaning as the number 27, which is the next to it in its own series of "compound" numbers.

37. This number has a distinct potency of its own. It is a number of good and fortunate friendships in love, and in combinations connected with the opposite sex. It is also good for partnerships of all kinds. It is a fortunate indication if it appears in connection with future events.

38. Has the same meaning as the number 29, which is the next to it in its own series of "compound" numbers.

39. Has the same meaning as the number 30, which is the next to it in its own series of "compound" numbers.

40. Has the same meaning as the number 31, which is next to it in its own series of "compound" numbers.

41. Has the same meaning as the number 32, which is next to it in its own series of "compound" numbers.

42. Has the same meaning as the number 24.

43. This is an unfortunate number. It is symbolised by the signs of revolution, upheaval, strife, failure, and prevention, and is not a fortunate number if it comes out in calculations relating to future events.

CHEIRO'S BOOK OF NUMBERS 85

44. Has the same meaning as 26.
45. Has the same meaning as 27.
46. Has the same meaning as 37.
47. Has the same meaning as 29.
48. Has the same meaning as 30.
49. Has the same meaning as 31.
50. Has the same meaning as 32.
51. This number has a very powerful potency of its own. It represents the nature of the warrior; it promises sudden advancement in whatever one undertakes; it is especially favourable for those in military or naval life and for leaders in any cause. At the same time it threatens enemies, danger, and the likèlihood of assassination.
52. Has the same meaning as 43.

We have now completed the 52 numbers which represent the 52 weeks of our year, and for all practical purposes there is no necessity to proceed further. I will now show my readers the method of employing the symbolism of these "compound" numbers, together with the "single" numbers whose meaning they have learned earlier in this book.

The rule to follow is: One must add the date one wishes to know about to the total of the compound numbers of one's name, see what number this gives one and read the meaning I have given to the added number.

EXAMPLE.—I will suppose you wish to know if, say, Monday the 26th April will be a favourable day for you to carry out some plan: let us say, to ask for a rise in your position or in your wages. Take the number given to each letter of your name from the alphabet I have shown you, add to the total "compound" number or its single digit the number given by the addition of the 26th April, 2 plus 6 an 8, add this 8 to the total of your Name number and Birth number and look up the meaning I have given to the final number produced, and you will find at once whether Monday, the 26th, will be favourable to you or not. If you see that it does not give a fortunate number, then add the next day, the 27th, or the next until you come to a date *that is indicated as favourable*. Act on the favourable date thus shown, and you will find that the day thus indicated will be fortunate for you.

86 CHEIRO'S BOOK OF NUMBERS

Suppose your name to be John Smith born 8th January, work the name out as follows:

```
J = 1                S = 3
O = 7                M = 4
H = 5                I = 1
N = 5                T = 4
    —                H = 5
   18 = 9                —
                        17 = 8
```

EXAMPLE.—You now add the 9 and the 8 together, which gives you the "compound" number of 17, whose units added together give 8. To this add the 8 produced by similar means from the 26th April, this gives you the number 16, with 7 for the single number; now add the Birth number 8th January to this 7 and you obtain 15 for the last compound number with 6 for the last single number.

Look up the meaning I have given to the compound Number 15: you will find it stated "for obtaining money, gifts, and favours from others, it is a fortunate number." Therefore the occult influences playing on John Smith, born 8th January, would be favourable on the 26th April for his using that date to ask favours or carry out his plans. If it had not given favourable indications "John Smith" should then work out the 27th April, or the next day or the next, until he found a date indicated as fortunate.

The same rule applies for every name and every date of birth.

CHAPTER XIV

MORE INFORMATION OF HOW TO USE "SINGLE" AND "COMPOUND" NUMBERS

FOLLOWING the publication of some articles I published in a leading London paper, I received some thousands of letters asking for further information as to how to make the Birth number and the Name number accord. I have, therefore, worked out the following example.

If possible, make the Birth number and the number given by the Name agree; the vibrations will then all be in harmony, and will give a greater promise of success if the number is a favourable one.

As an illustration, take again the example I gave in the previous chapter, of John Smith:

```
J = 1            S = 3
O = 7            M = 4
H = 5            I = 1
N = 5            T = 4
                 H = 5
---              ---
18 = 1 plus 8 = 9    17 = 1 plus 7 = 8
```

The single number of John totals a 9, and the single number of Smith equals an 8; the 8 and 9 added together make 17, and 1 plus 7 makes 8. The number of the entire Name is therefore an 8. If John Smith were born on any day making an 8, such as the 8th, 17th, or 26th of a month, the number of the Name and the number of the Birth *would then be in harmony*, and although the 8 is not such a lucky number to have in an ordinary way, yet in such a case there would be *no clash in the numbers*; and if John Smith, knowing this, used the dates making an 8, such as the 8th, 17th, or 26th, for his important transactions, he would find himself more fortunate.

If, on the contrary, he had another number, say 2, as his Birth number, such as the 2nd, 11th, 20th, or 29th, his Name and his Birth number would *not be in vibration one to the other*, and there would always be a muddle or jumble in his affairs, and he would also not be able to decide which number to act on or what date he should use.

As he cannot alter his Birth number, then the thing to do is to alter the *Name number*. If he added a letter making a 3 to his name, such as a C, a G, an L, or an S, which in the Alphabet I gave in a previous chapter have the number 3, and wrote his name, say, "John C. Smith," or "John G. Smith," and insisted on being known and called as that, this new Number 3, added to the 17, which John Smith made before, would now give a total of 20, or a single number of 2, and then both the Name number and the Birth number *would be in harmonious vibration together*, and he would also be sure that he would be right in selecting any date that makes a 2, such as the 2nd, 11th, 20th, or 29th of any month, as the most favourable day to make any change or carry out any important plan.

If, however, "John Smith" was born under an 8, such as the 8th, 17th, or 26th of any month, as the total of the numbers of his name also make an 8, I would then not advise him to add a letter or change the Name number, but to work under the 8, as I explained earlier.

Surely, this is a simple, clear rule, and will help those countless readers who may be puzzled as to how to get their Name number and Birth number to accord.

However, if a person is born under either of those peculiar numbers such as a 4 or an 8, and if the Name number should also total up to a 4 when one is born under an 8, or to an 8 when one is born under a 4, then for material success it would be better if one added some letter, as I explained in the case of John Smith, so that the total of your number is no longer a 4 or an 8, but one with a more fortunate vibration, making, say, a 1, 3, 6, or 9. Such a change in the majority of cases will produce most fortunate results and set up entirely new vibrations, which will change a lonely, unlucky life into one of happiness and success.

I would also strongly advise all those who have the combination of 4 and 8 when they make the change by altering their name to produce another number, such as a 1, 3, 6, or 9, to wear the colours and jewels I have set out for these numbers in an earlier chapter in this book dealing with "single" numbers, and I am absolutely confident that they will never regret having followed my advice.

I also advise that in order to get the best advantage out of one's numbers, that in living in cities and towns a person should select a house to live in whose number also gives the same vibration as the Birth and Name number. If they live in the country they should give a name to their house which produces the same number as the Birth and Name. Especially in the case of a person having an 8 for the Birth number and a 4 for the Name number, or vice versa, they should, under no circumstances, live in a house whose number worked out to the single digit of a 4 or an 8.

CHAPTER XV

WHY THE BIRTH NUMBER IS THE MOST IMPORTANT

THE Birth number is the easiest and clearest to use for everyday matters, and for all those who are not advanced students in occult symbolism. It indicates with authority and decision the exact date for action, namely a date which will be *in accord and harmony with the Birth number*, and the rules concerning it are simple and easy to understand.

A person born on, say, the 1st, 10th, 19th, or 28th, of any month will be quite safe in picking out any one of these dates as the best date for any important action. As the number 4 is what may be called the feminine or negative side of the 1, he or she can take this number as *an associate number*, but on account of the peculiar qualities of this number 1 I do not advise it to be chosen for any *worldly or material affairs*. This number 4 will generally be found by number 1 persons as coming into their lives "on its own," if I may be permitted to describe its action as such, but more in the nature of a fatalistic number which has an influence on their lives *outside of their control* and certainly not always connected with the happier side of life. In many instances of number 1 people in my collection, the number 4, such as the 4th, 13th, 22nd, and 31st, has brought on these dates the news of an accident, a death, or a sorrow which has played some important part in their lives. The number 1 people also often find that they seem unconsciously to be drawn to live in houses whose number makes a 4, such as a house in a terrace or street numbered 4, 13, 22, 31, 40, 49, etc., and although such houses may be proved to be associated with important events in the career, yet I have seldom found them associated with *material* advantages.

A person whose Birth number is an 8 should certainly never live in a house whose number makes a 4, 13, 22, 31, 40, etc., and neither should a person whose Birth number makes a 4 live in a house whose number makes an 8, 17, 26, 35, 44, etc., not, at least, if they wish to escape sorrow, misfortune, and strange fatality.

The second best numbers for a person whose Birth number makes a 1 are the interchangeable numbers of the 2–7, and dates these numbers make, such as the 2nd, 7th, 11th, 16th, 20th, 25th, or 29th, and houses under the numbers 2, 7, 11, 16, 20, 25, 29, 34, etc., are generally not unfavourable; but as these numbers are related to change or unsettled conditions, the number 1 person seldom settles down in houses under the 2–7 numbers, or finds conditions brought into his or her life under the dates given by these numbers as relating to *fixed or settled matters*.

Under the law of harmony and vibration, there is no question but that number 1 persons should be associated as much as possible with the same number in all its degrees; number 2 persons with the number 2 in all its forms. Persons born under the 3 should employ their number 3, and so on for all the numbers with the exception of those born under the 4 and the 8. In the latter cases I recommend, then, *not* to *increase* the peculiar influence of the 4 and 8, but to choose more fortunate vibrations.

This is where the power and knowledge of the Name number will apply. A number 4 or a number 8 person who desires to get under more fortunate vibrations, as they cannot alter their Birth number they can at least *change their Name number* and live under it and so become equally as fortunate as those whose Birth number is a lucky one.

I will give an example of what I mean.

Suppose a man or woman has been born on, say, the 8th, 17th, or 26th of January, and the Name number works out, let us say, to a final total of a 1, 3, 5, or 6 (I have purposely taken the strong or positive numbers). Then I most certainly advise the number 8 persons to drop using the 8 in all their transactions and use instead any strong number *the name may give*, such as a 1, 3, 5 or 6, and a number 4 person should do likewise.

You will notice I have not used the 9 in giving this rule, and my reason for not doing so is that the 4, which is the symbol of the Planet Uranus, and the 8, which represents the Planet Saturn, are so antagonistic in their qualities to the 9, the symbol of Mars, that it is better to keep such numbers apart.

This may sound strange to those who have not made any study of occultism, but believe me, the above rule is not laid down at random or by any shadowy guesswork; on the contrary, it has a solid foundation in the science of the Planets, and anyone who has ever studied Astrology will tell you that I am right when I say that any combination of the Planets of Mars (9) and Saturn (8) or Uranus (4) can only foreshadow troubles and disasters of all kinds.

To resume, the reason I advise that the Birth number is the most important as the Key to the main "fadic" number influencing the life is that in the first place *it is unalterable*; secondly, it is related to the planet's influence at the moment of birth, and thirdly, by some mysterious law of vibration—which, even if we do not understand, we must admit to exist even in such so-called inanimate objects as crystals, molecules, and atoms—the moment of birth decides the note of harmony or vibration, and so has its influence on the actions of our lives from the cradle to the grave.

Further, the Birth number relates to the material side of life, the Name number to the more occult or spiritual side of our existence.

Also the Name number is more difficult to be sure of—*it must be the product of the name we are most known by*. This presents a problem for the average man or woman. Many men are more known by their surnames than by their Christian and surname together, and many women are called by some "pet" name to the complete extinction of their Christian name. In working out such cases mistakes may easily be made and a number allotted which is not the true one, whereas by going by the Birth number and using it *as the foundation* no mistake can be made.

If, then, it is found that the name *one thinks* is the correct one, and if its number gives the same number or any degree of the same number as the Birth number, then one can be absolutely certain that no mistake is being made, for if both the Name number and the Birth number accord there is nothing one can desire better.

If the Name number does not accord with the Birth number, it can be made to agree by the addition of an initial or an alteration in the Christian name, so that both give the same vibration; and I advise this to be done in every case where the Birth and Name numbers do not agree, except in the case of the numbers 4 and 8 which I have spoken of earlier in this chapter.

Those who are advanced students in occult symbolism can utilise the hidden meaning given by both Christian and surnames to work out the finer shades of destiny, but for all ordinary cases—and I must not lose sight of the fact that I am writing this book for the average man and woman, those who want to help themselves in the easiest possible way, and who have, perhaps, no time for deep and abstruse study—to all those, I know I cannot do better than to advise them to follow closely the rules governing the Birth number as set out in these pages.

NOTE.—The number of the month of Birth or the year of Birth is not so *personal or so intimate* in regard to close calculations as is the number of the day of Birth.

The number of the month is useful as far as general matters, and the number of the year to the wider current of events.

EXAMPLE.—A person born, say, on the 6th June, 1866. Write this down in the following order:

6th   =   6   (Individual or Personal)
June   =   5   (General Matters)
1866   = 21 =   3   (Current of Destiny)

The numbers 6, 5, and 3 should be regarded as separate and distinct and not added together.

The year number totalled and added to itself indicates an important year in the Destiny.

Example   1866 = 21
                           21
                         ─────
                         1887

A further illustration of this is given later in the case of William I of Prussia.

CHAPTER XVI

SOME ILLUSTRATIONS OF NAMES AND NUMBERS

AS it is impossible in a book of this size to go into every shade of the occult significance of numbers that spring from the foundation of 1 to 9, I must confine myself to giving a few illustrations of how to use the numbers allotted to the letters of the Hebrew alphabet for the purpose of showing how Destiny appears interwoven with numbers and names.

The great Napoleon originally wrote his name as Napoleon Buonaparte. Later on in his life he changed it to Napoleon Bonaparte. This change had a curious significance:

>Napoleon equals in numbers a 5
>Buonaparte ,,   ,,   ,,   ,, 5

The number 5, as I showed earlier in these pages, is considered a magical number and was carried by the ancient Greeks as a mascot when they went into battle. The two numbers of 5, if added, producing 10, are equally important and strangely significant in this case.

When Napoleon altered the spelling to Bonaparte, it altered the vibration of this word to an 8, and if you refer to what I said about this number you will find on the lower plane it represents revolution, anarchy, waywardness, conflict with human justice, and on the lower plane a tragic ending to the life. Although a great man, Napoleon was on the lower plane of existence, as can be seen if one looks up how the number 8 (Saturn) and the 9 (Mars) dominated the chief events of his career. As Napoleon Bonaparte the two names total the number 13, which number, in the occult symbolism which accompanies this system of letters and numbers, bears the curious picture of a skeleton with a scythe *mowing men down*, also a symbol of "Power" which "if wrongly used will bring destruction upon itself."

This was so borne out by Napoleon's career that further comment is unnecessary.

Some remarkable illustrations of the significance of names and numbers may be had from examples of ships.

The United States battleship *Maine*, which so mysteriously exploded in Havana Harbour, and in which every man on board was lost, gives for the word "Maine" the number 16 for its compound number, the symbolism for this number being, as you have read on page 81, "A Tower Struck by Lightning." The mystery of the blowing up of this warship has never been solved, but it caused the declaration of war by the United States against Spain.

Another tragic ship disaster was that of the *Waratah*, which, after leaving Australia, sank with all her passengers and crew as if she had been swallowed up by the ocean. The number of the word "Waratah" equals 20, which, as you have read on page 82, is called "the Judgment." This number is symbolised by the figure of a winged angel sounding a trumpet, while from below a man, a woman, and a child are seen rising from a tomb with their hands clasped in prayer.

Yet another illustration might be taken from the fate of the *Leinster*, the Holyhead and Kingstown mail-boat that was torpedoed by a German submarine within sight of the Irish coast during the last months of the 1914–1918 War.

The word "Leinster" gives the compound number of 28, "a number full of contradictions," which also indicates "loss through trust in others." This boat was carrying a large number of soldiers as well as passengers, who certainly trusted their lives to others, in the belief that the boat would be accompanied by some of the destroyers from Kingstown Harbour. For some unexplained reason the order to the destroyers never came—the *Leinster* sailed alone, and in less than an hour met her fate and the loss of several hundred lives.

I know two men who at the last moment avoided going on that boat on that particular night by noticing that the compound numbers of their names made 28, the same number as the *Leinster*, and as they had read that in this system of symbolism it is not a fortunate number, and being struck by the coincidence of the name of the boat making the same number, both men took their luggage off at the last moment, and so escaped.

It is quite natural that under the tension of war people are more inclined to watch for the slightest clue that might give a warning of danger. I know of many instances where men actually saved their lives by following the clue given by this system of numbers. In one case a man resting by the side of his battery was amusing himself asking the birth dates of the men around him. He was startled to find that they were all born under the number 8, he himself being born on the 26th January, a number 8 man in the "period of the 8." It had just dawned on him that the day of the month also happened to be an 8, namely the 17th February, and looking up, he counted the number of the battery: *it was also an* 8. Just then a German gun opened fire. He counted the shells as they dropped, each one coming nearer and nearer. As the seventh fell he could not resist the dread that overcame him—he rushed out into the open, and as he did so, the eighth shell struck his battery—he was the only one who escaped.

CHAPTER XVII

EXAMPLES OF HOW NUMBERS RECUR IN LIVES

AMONG my collection on the influence of numbers in connection with events, I have many that are decidedly interesting.

The following letter relates to a curious coincidence concerning numbers:

DEAR SIR,—

I should like to give some facts about the No. 7. I was born on the 7th day of the 7th month; I was never ill until my 7th birthday, I never failed in an examination until my 7th, and the 7th girl I proposed to accepted me. Probably I was the 7th man who proposed to her.

I have an uncle who has been exceptionally unlucky in his experience of No. 8,631. His wife was killed in a railway accident in a carriage numbered 8,631; he himself broke a leg in a cab smash, the cab running into him being No. 8,631; and his four children died at the ages of 8, 6, 3, and 1 respectively.

Yours faithfully,
A. B. FRENCH.

SIR ALMA-TADEMA AND NUMBERS

The following appeared in many of the London newspapers:

Sir Alma-Tadema, the famous artist, says his important number is 17. He was 17 when he first met his wife; their first house had that number; it was on August 17th that the work of rebuilding his home began, and on November 17th that he took up his residence there. His second marriage was in 1871,—and here 17 is the result of the figures added together. His house, in the artistic quarter of St. John's Wood, was again a multiple of 17. Sir Alma-Tadema was born on January 8th, which would account for the 17th, which gives the single number 8, having such importance in his life.

King Edward VII and Numbers

King Edward was born on the 9th November in a month that is called in Astrology "the second house of Mars" and governed by 9, the number of Mars.

His marriage took place in the year 1863, which numbers added to the other make 9; he was to have been crowned on the 27th of June, which figures added together make 9, and he was actually crowned on August 9th.

King Edward often referred to me "as the man who would not let him live past 69." On the occasion when I first had the honour of meeting him as Prince of Wales in Lady Arthur Paget's house, he asked me to "work out his numbers." I did so and explained the reason his "fadic" or "root" numbers were the 6 and the 9. I then told him that when these two numbers came together would be his fatal year, and further that the event should take place on a day making the number 6 in a month governed by the 6, which would be May. He never forgot my prediction, and it is my melancholy privilege to record that the last occasion when I had any conversation with his late Majesty was a few weeks before his death. He was joining the royal train at Victoria to make his usual journey to the Continent when he noticed me, I happening also to be going abroad. He sent an equerry to call me, and he said, smiling broadly:

"Well, 'Cheiro,' I'm still alive, as you see, but from that warning of yours, as I am now in my 69th year, I must take care"—a reference to the fact that according to the fadic system of numbers his 69th year was for him a dangerous year. He then spoke briefly of his racing wagers, and concluded by emphasising how remarkably my advice had been crowned by success.

Alas, in a few short weeks he returned to Buckingham Palace, and the public heard with consternation of his illness, which proved fatal. On May 6th—in his 69th year, the first time that these "fadic" numbers came together—my prediction was fulfilled.

When I had the honour of a prolonged conversation with

his Majesty Edward VII some years previous to his death, he turned with peculiar interest to the subject of numbers and how curiously they seemed to "follow him about."

He told me that while in Berlin in 1889 he had had some conversation on the subject with a man named Streltz, a very noted occultist, who predicted many events in the life of the ex-Kaiser. But even Streltz did not seem able to explain to his royal inquirer the mystery of fadic or fatalistic numbers that appear to govern various lives. My various interviews with King Edward VII are gone into more fully in my book of Memoirs called *Confessions: Memoirs of a Modern Seer*.

KING EDWARD AND LORD RANDOLPH CHURCHILL

Incidentally, King Edward mentioned that his "dear friend," as he called him, Lord Randolph Churchill, was extremely superstitious in regard to the number 13, and attributed many adverse events to the fact that he was born on the 13th of February, 1849, the total of whose numbers 22 also made a 4.

I explained to King Edward that the idea that 13 was an unfortunate number was not supported by occultism; that it was in fact an important number if persons were born on the 4th, 13th, 22nd, or 31st, and it was simply regarded as ill-omened because in occultism it was looked upon with veneration.

A few years before his death in London in January, 1895, I had a brief interview with this famous statesman, and he reminded me that my theory of numbers had interested him very much. From King Edward he had gathered that I thought that 4 was his fadic number, and I confirmed this. It was also represented with almost all the leading events of his life.

LORD RUSSELL OF KILLOWEN

Another remarkable instance of prediction by numbers was in the case of my meeting with the then Sir Charles Russell. I explained to him that his important numbers were the 1 and the 4, with what are called their interchangeable numbers of 2 and 7, and that he would reach the highest position his career could give him on a date that made a 1, such as the 1st, 10th, 19th, or 28th in a month governed by the 2 and 7, such as July, which is governed by those numbers, and in a year whose number added up to the number of 4. He made a careful note of this, and when he wore his robes of Lord Chief Justice of England for the first time he sent for me to come to the Law Courts. After the ceremony of installation was over he came to me in his private room and as a souvenir gave me a signed impression of his hand.

CHAPTER XVIII

THE DREAD OF THE "13" UNFOUNDED

NEARLY all people have an extraordinary dread of the number 13, which, if they only knew the real truth, is not at all the unlucky number they imagine it to be.

The origin of this dread is due primarily to the fact that it was much used in connection with occultism, and was in far-off times regarded as a powerful although a fatalistic number. As I stated before in previous pages, in some of the old writings of famous Adepts it is said, "He who understands the number 13 hath the Keys of power and dominion."

The opposition of the early Church to occultism was one of the principal reasons why this number became "taboo." It was given out that as 13 sat down to the Last Supper it would be unlucky if 13 were to eat together, and that one of the 13 would die within the year, and so forth.

I must say I could never see the logic of this, for if Christ had not been crucified the Scriptures would not "have been fulfilled," in which case Christianity would never have existed.

There was another reason, however, why 13 was dreaded, and this was because the occult symbolism that stood for this number was represented by a mystic picture of "a skeleton with a scythe in its bony hands reaping down men."

It was a curious picture that few could understand, and those who did kept their knowledge to themselves in an age when even to speak of such things was to forfeit one's life by torture or at the stake.

This picture allotted to the number 13, although drawn or painted in many different ways, always contained the same idea: a skeleton reaping in a field, hands and feet springing up among new-grown grass, the crowned head of a man fallen at the point of the scythe, while a female head with flowing hair parted in the centre appeared in the background.

To find the true interpretation of this weird picture one must go back to the meaning attached to the single number 4, of which the 13 makes a second 4 in its compound number.

The single 4, as you have read earlier in these pages, is a strange number in itself. Persons dominated by it are usually misunderstood and lonely in their lives; people who bring about opposition with secret enemies constantly at work against them; they reverse the order of things in communities and governments; they are attracted to social questions and reforms of all kinds; they rebel against authority and set up new dynasties or republics.

The 13 has all these qualities in its higher scale, but even more accentuated. It cuts down all before it, reversing the order of things shown by the hands and feet springing up in the grass and the crowned head falling before the scythe. The female head in the background denotes social reform, the new order of things, and the uplifting of woman, and so forth.

It was perhaps this picture of a skeleton with a scythe in its bony fingers, calling up the idea of Death in the minds of those who could not understand the inner meaning of the symbolism, that caused the number 13 to be so dreaded.

If people will, however, only think, they will see that the 13 belongs to the series of 4, in the range of 4, 13, 22, 31, etc., and consequently a person born, say, on the 4th, 13th, 22nd, or 31st of a month will find all these numbers recurring in their careers, and this being so, the 13 will crop up just as often as the other numbers which make a 4.

In my collection about the continual recurrence of 13 in a career, the following instances are very remarkable:

Mr. H. C. Sherman, of Denver, Colorado, met, proposed, and was accepted by Miss Weeks on the 13th, and led her to the altar at 13 minutes past 10 on Friday, June 13th, 1913. The birthdays of the bride and bridegroom fell on the 13th. At the wedding there were 13 guests, and the bride carried 13 roses in her bouquet.

Police-Sergeant John Figg, in acknowledging a presentation from his comrades of the Dover Police Force on his retirement, reports the *Daily Express*, denied that ill-luck attached to the number 13. He said he was one of a family of 13; he started work at 13, was 13 years in his first employment, joined the Dover Police on April 13th, and his family numbered 13.

The fateful number 13 appears with strange significance in the circumstances surrounding the death of Mr. Phuvah Rudd, of North Burton, Yorks. Mr. Rudd fell down dead from heart disease on the 13th day of the month. He had been 13 weeks on the village club fund, had, on the day of his death, 13 shillings only left to draw; his youngest son attained his 13th birthday on the day of the funeral, which was attended by 13 members of the club, and by 13 members of the family, whose total mileage in travelling from their homes to the funeral amounted to 1300 miles. Mr. Rudd's family consisted of 13 members, including the eldest son, whose official number in the Royal Navy is 13, and who is at present serving on his 13th ship. Mr. Rudd's baptismal name of Phuvah appears only once in the Bible and that is in the 13th verse of the 46th chapter of Genesis. Thirteen telegrams were despatched from Hunmanby Telegraph Office announcing the death.

I do not know when this man was born, but with such a recurrence of the number 13 it is nearly certain that he must have been born on a date making a 4, such as the 4th, 13th, 22nd, or 31st.

Sir,—

I see your readers are interesting themselves in the number 13. I am a thirteener. I was born on January 13th, 1840 (the last figures adding up to 13). I began to earn money at 13 and I made my first political speech when I was 26 (twice 13), and on January 26th (again twice 13) a speech which was the beginning of my political fortunes. It was the 13th year after my first essay at entering the Sunderland Town Council before I was elected as M.P. for the town. I enjoyed my first wife's companionship only 13 years, and she died on the 26th of a month. I was for three years Mayor of Sunderland and for 10 Chairman of the Durham County Council, or 13 in all. I married my second wife when I was 58 (the figures added make 13) and in 1898 (which figures added come to twice 13). She was born on the 13th of a month and died on a 13th.

I was an active member of the Liberal Party for thrice thirteen years, and left it in order to support Mr. Chamberlain's Tariff Reform crusade in 1903 (which figures add up to 13). At the Tariff Reform election at Sunderland my successful poll totalled 12,334 which figures added together make 13. Important and fortunate events in my life occurred when I was 13, twice 13, thrice 13, and four times 13.

You will thus see that I am very much of a thirteener, and that the number has carried with it for me good and evil fortune.

Yours, etc.

SAMUEL STOREY.

SOUTHILL, CHESTER-LE-STREET,
December 13th.

FEAR OF THIRTEEN

Not only the ignorant have a fear of the thirteen [says the *Chronicle*]. Where in the world could one find a greater body of miscellaneous knowledge than among the frequenters of the reading-room at the British Museum? Yet never, probably, in the history of the reading-room have the seats numbered 13, from A13 to T13, all have been full at once. And those of the thirteens that do find occupants always find them last. The majority of readers prefer a little bare supplementary table to a palatial desk when that desk has the fatal number above it.

In many hotels, even the modern ones, there is no Room 13; and a similar peculiarity characterises the seats of opera-houses in Italy.

But the dread of 13 has only a limited geographical range.

In the East and in the West the number is honoured. In the Indian Pantheon there are 13 Buddhas. The mystical discs which surmount Indian and Chinese pagodas are 13 in number. Enshrined in the Temple of Atsusa, in Japan, is a sacred sword with 13 objects of mystery forming its hilt. Turning westward, 13 was the sacred number of the Mexicans. They had 13 snake gods.

The original States that formed the American Union were 13; its motto, *E Pluribus Unum*, has 13 letters, the American eagle has 13 feathers in each wing, and when George Washington raised the Republican standard he was saluted with 13 guns. These facts dealing with the U.S.A. are fully set out in *Cheiro's World Predictions*.

CHAPTER XIX

THE EXTRAORDINARY EXAMPLE OF NUMBERS IN THE LIVES OF ST. LOUIS AND LOUIS XVI

ONE of the most remarkable instances I have ever come across of numbers pointing to a sequence of similar events in lives as far apart as over five hundred years, and which might be used as evidence of reincarnation, is the extraordinary case of St. Louis of France and King Louis XVI, which was published in 1852 in a book called *Research into the Efficacy of Dates and Names in the Annals of Nations*.

As history shows, there was an interval of exactly 539 years between the birth of St. Louis and Louis XVI.

If one adds this interval number to the remarkable dates in the life of St. Louis, a parallel of events, even to similarity in names, will be seen in the events in the life of Louis XVI.

St. Louis		Louis XVI
Birth of St. Louis 23rd April,	1215	Birth of Louis XVI 23rd August,
Add interval	539	
	1754	1754
Birth of Isabel, sister of St. Louis	1225	Birth of Elizabeth, sister of Louis XVI
Add interval	539	
	1764	1764
Death of Louis VIII, father of St. Louis,	1226	Death of the Dauphin, father of Louis XVI
Add interval	539	
	1765	1765

CHEIRO'S BOOK OF NUMBERS

St. Louis	Louis XVI
Minority of St. Louis commences 1226	Minority of Louis XVI commences
Add interval 539	
1765	1765
Marriage of St. Louis 1231	Marriage of Louis XVI
Add interval 539	
1770	1770
Majority of St. Louis (King) 1235	Accession of Louis XVI, King of France
Add interval 539	
1774	1774
St. Louis concludes a peace with Henry III 1243	Louis XVI concludes a peace with George III
Add interval 539	
1782	1782
An Eastern prince sends an ambassador to St. Louis desiring to become a Christian 1249	An Eastern prince sends an ambassador to Louis XVI for the same purpose
Add interval 539	
1788	1788
Captivity of St. Louis 1250	Louis XVI deprived of all power
Add interval 539	
1789	1789
St. Louis abandoned 1250	Louis XVI abandoned
Add interval 539	
1789	1789

St. Louis

Birth of Tristan (sorrow)   1250
Add interval   539
                            ─────
                             1789

Beginning of Pastoral under
  Jacob   1250
Add interval   539
                            ─────
                             1789

Death of Isabel d'Angoulême 1250
Add interval   539
                            ─────
                             1789

Death of Queen Blanche,
  mother of St. Louis   1253
Add interval   539
                            ─────
                             1792

St. Louis desires to retire and
  become a Jacobin   1254
Add interval   539
                            ─────
                             1793

St. Louis returns to Madeleine
  en Provence   1254
Add interval   539
                            ─────
                             1793

Louis XVI

Fall of the Bastille and Commencement of the Revolution.

1789

Beginning of the Jacobins in France

1789

Birth of Isabel d'Angoulême in France

1789

End of the White Lily of France

1792

Louis XVI quits life at the hands of the Jacobins

1793

Louis XVI interred in the cemetery of the Madeleine in Paris

1793

This, I believe, is one of the most curious examples of history repeating itself at a fixed interval. The addition of the interval number 539 reduced to the single digit gives the number 8, and the number of letters in the name LOUIS XVI gives also the 8. This number, as I explained earlier, represents the symbol of Justice and of one appealing from the brutality of Human Justice to that of the Divine.

CHAPTER XX

PERIODICITY IN NUMBERS

THE Law of Periodicity is shown in some lives in a very remarkable manner. In many cases it may last for hundreds of years, as may be noticed in the lives of St. Louis and Louis XVI in the interval of 539 years that separated these two Kings of France, and which interval, when added to the date of important events in St. Louis's life, repeated similar events in the career of Louis XVI. This is considered one of the most curious examples known in history.

Further, it will be noticed that St. Louis was born on April 23rd, the numbers added together producing a 5. Louis XVI was born August 23rd, also producing a 5.

These names worked out by the Hebrew Alphabet are:

```
SAINT       LOUIS
3 1 1 5 4   3 7 6 1 3
—————       —————
  14 = 5      20 = 2
            5 and 2 = 7

LOUIS       XVI
3 7 6 1 3    16
—————       ——
  20 = 2      7
            2 and 7 = 9
```

The name Saint Louis worked out to its single digit gives 7, the spiritual number. Louis XVI worked out to its single digit gives 9, the material number. These two single numbers added together give 16 for the compound number, the occult meaning being, as you have read in a previous chapter, "A Tower Struck by Lightning from which a man is falling with a Crown on his head," a fitting symbol in every sense for the downfall of Louis XVI.

After this date, the execution of Louis XVI, in 1793, we cannot yet trace this curious law of periodicity further, but in adding the interval number again to 1793 we get the year 2332, in which perhaps another incarnation of St. Louis will again reign in France.

Another interesting example of a number being associated with the Kings of France is the following:

The first King of France named Henri was consecrated on the *14th* May, 1029, and the last King of the name of Henri was assassinated on the *14th* May, 1610.

Fourteen letters it will be found make the name of Henri de Bourbon, who was the *14th* King to bear the title of King of Francè and Navarre.

On the *14th* December, 1553, or 14 centuries, 14 decades, and 14 years after the birth of Christ, Henri IV of France was born; the figures of the date 1553 added together make also the number 14.

On the *14th* May, 1554, Henri II signed the decree for the enlargement of the Rue de la Ferronnerie. The cause of this order—the narrowness of this street—not having been carried into execution, brought about the assassination of Henri IV *in that same street exactly 4 times 14 years later*.

On the *14th* May, 1552, Marguerite de Valois, the first wife of Henri IV, was born.

On the *14th* May, 1588, the Duke of Guise opened the revolt against Henri III.

On the *14th* March, 1590, Henry IV won the important Battle of Ivry.

On the *14th* May, 1590, the main Army of Henry IV was defeated at the Fauxbourg of Paris.

On the *14th* November, 1590, "the Sixteen" took an oath of death rather than serve Henri IV.

On the *14th* November, 1592, the French Parliament accepted the Papal Bull, which gave authority to the legate of Rome to nominate a king instead of Henri IV.

On the *14th* December, 1599, the Duke of Savoy submitted to Henry IV.

On the *14th* September, the Dauphin, who later became Louis XIII, was baptised.

On the *14th* May, 1610, owing to the narrowness of the Rue de la Ferronnerie, previously referred to, the street his father Henri II had planned to be enlarged, the carriage of the King was stopped by a cart which gave Ravaillac the opportunity to assassinate him.

On the *14th* May, 1643, Louis XIII, the son of Henri IV, died, on the same day of the same month that his father was killed, and if the figures of 1643 are added together they make the Number *14*, which had played such an important part in his father's career.

Louis XIV ascended the throne in 1643, also a *14*, and died in 1715, which also makes a *14*. His age at his death was 77, again making by addition a *14*.

Louis XV ascended the throne in 1715 = *14*.

Louis XVI was in the *14th* year of his reign when he convoked the States-General, which brought about the Revolution and his downfall.

The Restoration of the Bourbons took place in 1814, the number of this year added together making *14*.

The reason why this number 14 or its single number 5 appears so much associated with the destiny of France may be traced to the fact that in Astrology Paris has always been represented as governed by the Sign Virgo, whose Planet is Mercury in its negative aspect, whose number is a 5.

During the period of French history I have cited, Paris was the principal point of power. The king who reigned in Paris ruled in France.

The addition of important dates often appears to bring out subsequent dates of equal importance.

The following is a striking illustration from French history:

Revolution in France and fall of Robespierre
took place in 1794
The numbers of this date added together give . 21

CHEIRO'S BOOK OF NUMBERS

The fall of Napoleon	1815
1815 added gives	15
Fall of Charles X and Revolution in France	1830
1830 added gives	12
Death of the King Louis Philippe	1842
1842 added gives	15
End of Crimean War	1857
1857 added gives	21
The famous Treaty of Berlin	1878
1878 added gives	24
Danger of War with England over Fashoda	1902
1902 added gives	12
World War I	1914
1914 added gives	15
A date which was another crisis in French history	1929

Another curious example of the addition of dates, much commented on in both Berlin and Paris during 1914, is as follows:

In 1849, William I of Prussia fled with his mother, Queen Louise, and took refuge in England. Meeting with a woman well versed in Numerology, he asked her to tell him his future. "Add," she answered, "the figures of this important year together   1849

22

1871

In the year produced by this addition you will end a great war and will be proclaimed Emperor."

"And then———?" asked the King.

"Add 1871," she replied, "and you will get the year of your death." The King made the addition and wrote 1888.

"And what of my country after that?" the King asked.

"Add again," she answered, "and see what the total is."

The King added 1888

$$\frac{25}{1913}$$

"In that year," the woman said, "the man who wears your crown will prepare another war, which will bring about his ruin and that of your country, for the time being."

This story was repeated to me by a close relative of the ex-Kaiser when he visited me in Paris in 1904.

In Rome there is a very ancient tradition which says that no Pope who occupies the Chair of St. Peter can reign longer than 25 years. The Popes who came very near this strangely set period were the following:

Pius VI	who reigned	24 years	6 months	and	14 days
Adrian I	„ „	23 „	10 „	„	17 „
Pius VII	„ „	23 „	5 „	„	6 „
Alexander III	„ „	21 „	11 „	„	23 „
Sylvester I	„ „	21 „	0 „	„	4 „

Leo XIII entered his 25th year as Pope, but did not pass beyond the set period, although he occupied the Chair of St. Peter longer than any of his predecessors.

English history also contains many equally strange examples of numbers and dates reappearing continually in remarkable lives.

On the 29th May, 1630, Charles II was born.
 „ „ 29th „ 1660, he was restored to the Throne.
 „ „ 29th „ 1672, his fleet was destroyed by the Dutch.
 „ „ 29th „ 1679, the Covenanter Rebellion broke out.

On the 3rd September, Cromwell was born.
 „ „ 3rd „ won the Battle of Dunbar.
 „ „ 3rd „ he won the Battle of Worcester.
 „ „ 3rd „ he died.

In a previous chapter I have related the curious influence the numbers 6 and 9 had in the life of King Edward VII.

CHAPTER XXI

SOME ADDITIONAL INFORMATION

IN this volume I will endeavour to answer many enquiries from those interested in Numerology and give as much additional information as possible.

As there are many books on this subject that have appeared in the last few years which are not in accordance with some of the rules brought forward by me, I think it is only right to explain the chief fault to be found in the books of many writers on this subject is, that they have modelled their theories on literature that has appeared in different times or have copied what has been written and have not themselves had practical experience in proving the various theories from a wide variety of cases from actual life, and so have endeavoured to lay down rules which have no real foundation.

In my own case I have not only had long years of individual practice, but my articles in the Press and *Cheiro's Book of Numbers* on this subject have brought me many thousands of letters in which my correspondents have given the most detailed instances of how and under what circumstances they have proved certain numbers intimately associated with the important events of their lives. I know from such experience that the system I teach in my writings is a practical one and not simply theoretical.

The trouble with the majority of writers on occult subjects is, that they start off with the idea that they must clothe the truth they propose to write about with so many "frills" and "fancies" that the ordinary "man in the street" becomes lost in a labyrinth of vague theories and is left no wiser in the end than he was at the beginning.

To put matters briefly, the two schools of philosophy in regard to the subject of numbers are the Pythagorean and the more ancient one known as the Chaldean.

The Greek philosopher, Pythagoras, imbibed all his knowledge of the occult value of numbers during his residence in Egypt. On his return to Greece he established a school of occult philosophy that was eminently suited to the needs of his day. In this school only a very limited number of initiates were allowed to enter. The more involved and difficult the teachings became, the fewer were the favoured ones who could boast that they were the "chosen of the Master," consequently a kind of occult hierarchy was established that raised an insurmountable barrier between these students and those they were pleased to call "the common people."

From this the most involved and complicated system of occult philosophy became launched; nothing was allowed to be put in writing, knowledge had to be handed down by word of mouth, the most elaborate ceremonials were instituted in which initiates were sworn to secrecy, and the greatest efforts were made to conceal occult knowledge in every possible way.

After the death of Pythagoras, his many followers started schools of philosophy of their own. All of them differed widely as to what "the Master" really did teach. In the end confusion became still more confounded by the action of the early Fathers of the Christian Church condemning all occult learning as the "work of the devil."

One of the greatest of Pythagoras' teachings was that of the occult value of numbers. He laid down the axiom that numbers concealed and contained the secret of the universe. In this theory he was undoubtedly right, but his followers so complicated the rules he taught that in the end few could follow the great truth that underlay his wisdom.

In later years one can take a similar illustration from that wonderful teacher, Jesus of Nazareth. After his crucifixion his twelve disciples spread his teachings in various ways in accordance with their own mental inclination; following them the thousand and one popes, bishops, priests and deacons have added or subtracted from the teachings of "the Master" until in the end the vast majority of the people do not know what to follow or believe.

In the study of numbers I advocate that the students should endeavour to get back to the original source; that is why I claim that in returning to the original Chaldean, Hindu, and Hebrew system, which I teach in my books, one has more likelihood of arriving at the real truth of such studies.

I could easily write an entire volume on the history of numbers, tracing its origin from the most remote ages; but in this practical period of humanity I realise that such an elaborate treatise is not required—that what men and women want is the practical appeal to their own personal experience and nothing more.

It is for this reason I have written *Cheiro's Book of Numbers* for the masses, more than for the more limited erudite student. In this work I have followed the same idea, giving the more simple facts relating to the occult side of numbers, leaving the higher philosophy to those who have the leisure and disposition to solve the finer meanings for themselves.

I may be criticised, it is true, for this way of looking at things, but I believe in teaching "the people" more than "the person." Out of "the people" can always come some one individual who, by prolonged study and application, may develop into "a Master," and so lead on "from our dead selves to higher things."

Out of the many thousands of letters I have received, I shall now endeavour to answer the questions which appear to me as the most important.

"Should the words Mr., Mrs., or Miss be calculated when working out the complete number of a name?"

Answer: As I have explained before, it is *"the name one is most known by"* that should be used in working out the number of a name.

If, for example, a young lady is always addressed or spoken of as, say, Miss Jones—as is often the case in a large business establishment—then in connection *with that business* in which she is employed, Miss Jones should certainly take that name as the one she is most known by and work out the number of the name "Miss Jones" and use it, *but only in relation to the business she is employed in.* It is, in fact, her "trade name"; but for her home life or her private affairs she should work out the Christian name she is called by or the "pet" name she is known under. When the same young lady enters the state of matrimony and becomes "Mrs." she should then work out the numbers for her new title, but always keeping the numbers of her Christian or "pet" name *for her home and private life.* The same rule applies to every woman known and called continually "Mrs. Smith" or "Mrs. Jones," as the case may be, in the circle of friends or acquaintances in which she is called "Mrs."

Men in business for themselves or in large establishments, who are generally called "Mr." before their name, should also follow the above rule.

When a man or woman has many Christian names, they should only take the number made by the principal one— that they *are most known by*.

The same rule applies to every prefix or title a man or woman may obtain *by right of birth* or *as an honour*.

A good illustration of this is the case of the famous Melba.

The great diva's surname worked out to the compound number of 15, with 6 for the single, both being excellent for success. In one of my Press articles, speaking of the number 15, I said: "If this number is associated with a good or fortunate single number, it can be very lucky and powerful. It is peculiarly associated with 'good talkers' and often with gifts of eloquence, music, art and strong personal magnetism." All these qualities were characteristic of the great Melba, as she was called all through her successful career.

Her signature, Nellie Melba, produces the number 10, also a fortunate number, and the single number 1, which is a number of strong individuality and ambition. It also denotes that people possessing this num er have the desire to become the head or chief in whatever profession or occupation they take up.

If the number of her title, "Dame," which is the lucky number of 5, be added to the name Nellie Melba, the total of the last digits are: Dame 5, Nellie 4, Melba 6, giving again the compound number 15, so that as long as this famous woman existed good fortune always favoured her.

I will now give an example of a title which produces one of the unfortunate numbers, the curious effect it foreshadows as far as the promise of good luck is concerned.

In cases where the addition of the number of the title produces a 4 or an 8, it foreshadows that the fortunate numbers of the name have ceased their luck or power, and in such cases the title will become a detriment and not a happiness.

An illustration which may be given in connection with this is that of Napoleon. This name works out to the compound number of 41, which, as I state in my writings, is "a magical number usually associated with combinations of peoples or nations." The single number is a 5, also fortunate. When Napoleon became Emperor of France his name became Napoleon I, the 1 making his compound number 42 with the single number of 6. Both of these again are numbers of power and good fortune and he went down to posterity as the Great Napoleon.

In the case of Napoleon III the compound number becomes 44, which I stated in my articles "is a number of the gravest warnings for the future; it foreshadows disasters brought about by association with others and bad advice" —exactly what happened to Napoleon III. Again, the single number of his name became an 8. Even the magic of the name Napoleon was overshadowed by it, and Napoleon III went down to posterity as "the man who lost France."

I think these illustrations will help to show how a prefix to a name, or a title acquired or inherited, fits in with this wonderful science of Numerology, and the number it gives added to the other numbers is a further indication of good or evil fortune for the future.

The titles given to kings and queens when they ascend the throne, especially when taken in connection with their birth number, is generally very interesting.

In the case of King Edward VII, he changed his name when he came to the throne from Albert to Edward, the name he took working out as follows:

```
King    . . . . . . .   11 = 2
Edward  . . . . . . .   22 = 4
VII     . . . . . . .      = 7
                          ──
                          13
```

I have described this number in a previous chapter as a number of warning with its strange symbolism of "a skeleton" or "death."

It was certainly a warning of great changes that were about to occur in England, and taken in conjunction with his birth number, November 9th, by adding the 4 produced by the 13 to the 9, they again made a 13, which doubled the warning and also indicated a short reign.

In the case of King George V, the numbers produced are as follows:

```
King    . . . . . . .   11 = 2
George  . . . . . . .   25 = 7
V       . . . . . . .      = 5
                          ──
                          14 = 5
```

The compound number 14 I have already described in previous pages as "a number of movement, combinations of people and things, but danger from natural forces such as tempests, water, air, or fire, but with a strong element of risk and danger attached to it, generally owing to the actions and foolhardiness of others."

Born on June 3rd, the late King's birth took place in the Zodiacal Sign of Gemini, which is called the 1st House of Air. Consequently the dangers foreshown by the compound number of the name and title are all the more accentuated;

therefore the King's greatest danger came from anything in connection with air, even His Majesty's lungs, as the breathing apparatus of his system, come under this symbol of the Zodiacal Sign of Birth.

London, the capital of England, is also under the same sign of Gemini, and the greatest danger to it is from the air.

It is a curious fact and doubtless one charged with deep significance that not only George V but Queen Mary and the Duke of Windsor were all born under the sign of Gemini, or very close to it, in the 1st House of Air, and in the district of London, also under the same sign.

Although she has other Christian names, the Queen is always popularly known as Queen Mary. The numbers of her name are:

```
Queen  . . . . . . .  22 = 4
Mary   . . . . . . .     = 8
                        ─────
                        12 = 3
```

The compound number of this name is 12. In my previous chapters I have given the symbolism of this number as 'a number indicating anxiety of mind." It is also called 'the sacrifice." As Queen Mary was born on May 26th, her birth number is an 8, and in the name Queen Mary the 4 and the 8 are also produced.

These illustrations of the significance of titles and prefixes to a name will, I think, be useful to my readers and will answer some thousands of letters I have received asking for information on this point.

NOTE.—The Prince of Wales (The Duke of Windsor), born 10 p.m., June 23rd, 1894, at White Lodge, Richmond Park, London, is in what is called the "cusp" of Gemini-Cancer.

The sun at this date had just passed out of Gemini and was in 2 degrees 21 of Cancer.

The qualities of Gemini will be the main influence through his life.

His Majesty King George V, born June 3rd, 1865, 1.18 a.m., Marlborough House, London, has the sun in 12 degrees 25 of Gemini.

Her Majesty Queen Mary, born May 26th, 1867, 11.59 p.m., Kensington Palace, London, is in the "cusp" of Taurus-Gemini and has the sun in 5 degrees 13 of Gemini.

CHAPTER XXII

HOW TO FIND THE "LUCKY" DAY

IN answer to many letters from readers of *Cheiro's Book of Numbers*, I take this opportunity of explaining a point of very great importance, namely, how to find the "lucky" day.

I have stated that the birth number is the most important when the individual wants *to carry out his own plans*.

For example: A person we will say born on the 1st of a month will find *for all general purposes* that if he or she will use all dates making the Number One series, such as the 1st, 10th, 19th or 28th of any month, especially during what is called the "period of the 1" and "the period of the 2," namely, from June 21st to July 20th (period of the 2), and from July 21st to August 20th (period of the 1), they will have a far better chance of carrying out their plans successfully than if they did not follow this rule and did not know what dates to use for the best.

This is quite independent of any other rule, and I strongly recommend it.

To get a still more powerful vibration, I have advised that persons should try to make the number of their name (when they have worked out the letters of it by what is called the Mystic or Ancient Hebrew Alphabet) the same series as the number that is given by their birth date, and I have explained in a previous chapter how to do this by adding a letter to their name or taking away a letter, as the case may be. If these two numbers agree or are in harmony with one another, then they should use the date that is given to commence anything important, or endeavour to carry out their plans on that number which is indicated. They must, however, bear in mind that any number of the series they belong to is equally important.

EXAMPLE.—The person born on the 1st of the month will find the 10th, 19th, or 28th of equal importance to the number 1 on which they were born, and so on with every other birth number.

Naturally, when people begin to follow this idea, they must not expect to find their luck change in an instant, as if by magic. I have several letters before me as I write, where the writers expected their "luck" to change for the better within twenty-four hours. A few months ago there was one man who wrote that "at the end of a week he had found no change in his bad luck," but at the end of three months the same man again wrote to say that towards the middle of the third month he began to notice a distinct improvement in all his affairs.

Some of the writers have also apparently not grasped the example I gave in working out the number of the name of a man I called "John Smith." I stated in a previous chapter that if "John Smith" wanted to find out a favourable date to ask his employer for an increase in his wages he should add the numbers given by the name "John Smith" together, then add the single number of the date he wanted to know about and lastly to add his birth number. The result was a total of 15 as the last compound number with 6 as the last single number. I said, "Look up what I have given as the symbolism of the 15, and you will find it stated 'for obtaining money, gifts and favours from others it is a fortunate number,'" and therefore the date "John Smith" wanted to see his employer would be a favourable date for him to make his request.

This was given only as an illustration of finding out if one particular date would be likely to be favourable *for that special purpose*, but I never intended this to be employed to the exclusion of the other definite rule for *continual action all through the year* on the series given by the Birth number, such as for a number 1 person to use all dates that make a 1, as the 1st, 10th, etc.

It will be noticed that in the latter case the rule is *individual or personal*; in the "John Smith" case another life, namely the employer, was also concerned, and in consequence the rule given would not work out with such certainty.

CHAPTER XXIII

MORE INFORMATION ABOUT COLOURS AND NUMBERS

JUDGING from the large number of letters asking for more information as to colours and numbers, it appears that many readers are confused as to the colours given according to the number of the month and those given to the number of the day of birth.

There is no reason for anyone to get confused between the colours given by the number of the month and those given by the number of the day, if one will bear in mind that the number of the month is not as *close or intimate in its relationship to the individual* as is the colour indicated by the number of birth.

Take the month of January, for example. The "period of the number 8" as set out in my *Book of Numbers* (p. 58) is from December 21st to January 20th *in its positive aspect*, and from January 21st to February 21st *in its negative aspect*. The number 8, as I state in my book, has for its colours "all shades of dark grey, dark blue, and purple." In my other book, *When Were You Born?* I gave the same colours with the addition of "violet," and under the heading of "colours of the number 8" in the same book I have extended the list slightly by giving "all tones of dark greys, blues, browns, and russet shades." For the lucky jewels I have given "all dark stones, such as dull rubies, carbuncles, and the deep-toned sapphire, which is most markedly the jewel of the number 8." In the same book for persons born under a 4, I have given "all shades of grey and fawn and electric shades and the minor tints of yellow and green." In this more recently published *Book of Numbers* I have simply condensed the colours for the number 4 people to what are called "half shades, half tones, or electric colours," and have stated that "electric blues" and greys seem to suit them best of all. In all this there is no contradiction of terms, as the writers of many letters to me appear to imagine, but owing to the fact that in my last book my theme was principally numbers, I had to give more information on that part of the subject and less space to the colours. There are so many sides to the study of the occult value of numbers that one cannot put all the information in one book.[1]

The following information will, I think, be useful, and I am giving it in order to clear up a point which I have noticed in many of the letters that have been received.

Namely: A person born on, say, January 6th has read in my book *When Were You Born?* that January is the "period of the 8," and that the colours for the number 8 are "all tones of grey, all ranges of violet and purple, also black." Many of those who have written to me are puzzled to know whether they should use the colours of the 8 or those belonging to the number 6. My answer is, *employ most decidedly in such a case* the colours of the number 6 as the principal, individual, and "lucky" colours to use, but as the person was born in the "period of the 8" he or she can use, if they wish, *but as secondary* colours, those given by the number 8.

Another illustration I will give is for those born in the "period of the 9," namely between March 21st to April 27th, which is *the positive period of the* 9, and those born *in its negative period*, namely, between October 21st and November 27th.

If one will look up in my books the colours I have given to the number 9, they will find that they are "all shades of crimson or red, all rose tones and pink" for the *positive period*, while for the *negative period* in my book *When Were You Born?* if one reads about the period October-November, one will notice I say "all shades of *crimson and* blue."

Where does blue come in? one may ask.

Because *the opposite Sign of the Zodiac* to the period October 21st to November 27th is what is called "*the House of Venus*" in her positive aspect, and as Venus, which is also the number 6, represents in this wonderful colour scheme

[1] The deep-toned sapphire is also the principal jewel of the number 4, and all its series.

of nature all shades of blue, these blue rays appear to cross from one side of the Zodiac to the other and so become a favourable colour for persons born in the *negative period of the number* 9, as well as "all shades of crimson."

Going back to the "periods of the number 9" for a moment we find the basic colours for both these periods are red, crimson and pink, but the same rule applies as it did it my example for the "period of the 8." A person born on a 6, such as on the 6th, 15th, or 24th *in the period of the* 9, would have as his or her *principal colour* all shades of blue, with red, crimson, or pink, as his or her *secondary colours*.

The same rule applies to every month in the year and to every date of birth. It is quite simple when one has once grasped this principle and can appreciate the marvellous harmony of this wonderful universe in which we live.

CHAPTER XXIV

THE VALUE OF CONCENTRATION IN REGARD TO ONE'S NUMBER

IN order to help my readers to make the best of whatever their number may be, I will now give advice which I am sure will be found of great assistance to those who want to try to make the most of their lives.

Once the principal or dominating number of the life has been found, then the next step is *to increase its power as much as possible*, the exception being those who are born under the 8, namely the 8th, 17th, or 26th of any month, to whom I will give advice on this point later.

This increase of power can be obtained by employing one of the *greatest forces* that man is endowed with, namely the Power of Concentration.

There are very few people who know anything about this extraordinary power.

All successful men and women are endowed with it, many use it unconsciously. Some are born with it, others develop it, but the majority of mankind do not use it at all.

One may often have noticed the feeble, "wishy-washy" way most people talk. One may have tried hard to follow some rambling statement, but have found at the end that one hardly knows "what it was all about," or that the person who has tried to interest you has made no impression on you whatever. This has been due to the fact that the man or woman has no power of concentration, and consequently *no force behind their flow of words*.

It is the same when such people write a letter—again there may be a lot of words, even expressions and sentences well put together, but the letter has *no effect on you*, and very likely you toss it aside and think no more about it.

On the contrary, another person may say only a few words, but *those words take effect*; or they may write, and their sentences strike home—the secret of this mystery is *concentration of mind*.

The simplest way of developing this power is by the use of numbers. I will now explain.

The first thing to be done is to find one's own number, the birth number being in every case the simplest and the most certain; the next is to grasp *the meaning of that number*, and lastly, to think of oneself as if that number *belonged* to one, represented one, and were *part and parcel of one's aims and plans*.

This is the sure foundation on which to build.

We will now go a step farther. The man or woman who has found his own distinct number should plan with firm determination to use that number in every way possible.

They should mentally look forward to the day or date when their number is to appear and plan that *on that day* they will take a certain course of action, and when that day or date arrives that they will go straight for what they want without shilly-shallying or hesitation of any kind.

Having read previous chapters on numbers, the reader has by now grasped the characteristics of other persons that are born under their own or other numbers. It is quite a simple matter to find out the day of the month on which the person one is going to interview was born, for if one does not ask the year of birth, even the woman most sensitive about her age will tell the date on which she was born.

A number 1 person will realise how useless it is to attempt to dominate a number 3 person. On the contrary, they must appeal to their ambition, their conscientiousness in carrying out their duties, their love of order and discipline, their sense of independence and the pride of honour and self that is the foundation principle of the number 3 person.

If they bear this in mind, *concentrating at the same time on their own plan* that made them seek the interview they will find that the number 3 person, instead of being difficult to approach, will, on the contrary, be willing to help and will most probably give ideas and suggestions that will be useful.

Having chosen a date for the interview on *one of their own numbers*, and by doing so, having concentrated their mind on this plan of action, they will find how easily they will be able to influence the person they have come to interview.

CHAPTER XXV

COMBINATIONS BETWEEN I HYPHEN 4 PERSONS AND ADVICE TO THOSE BORN UNDER THE NUMBERS 4 AND 8

FOLLOWING the illustrations I gave in the previous chapters on the usefulness of concentration on one's own number, so as to increase its power (except in case of those born under the 4 and 8), we will now take as an example a number 1 person meeting another of his own number. My readers have already learned from previous articles that people born on the same series are naturally sympathetic to one another, and such knowledge gives the feeling in the first place that the other number 1 he is talking to is "one of themselves," as it were. This very sentiment radiating outwards destroys nervousness and allows the lines of human magnetism to vibrate in harmony from one to the other.

Let us now suppose that the number 1 person has arranged an interview with an individual born under the 2 series. In such a case he or she can select any date of the 1 or 2 series, such as the 1st, 2nd, 10th, 11th, 19th, 20th, 28th, or 29th. The number 1 person has read that number 2 persons have the feminine qualities of the number 1, and that, though opposite in character, the vibrations of both 1 and 2 persons are harmonious, and that they make good combinations. With this knowledge in his possession the number 1 person will make the effort to combine with the ideas of number 2, and so happy and good results will be obtained.

A number 1 and a number 4 person will also meet on a sympathetic and harmonious vibration for the reason that in Numerology the number 1 is always associated with the 4 and these numbers are written as 1 hyphen 4, and 4 hyphen 1, but as all number 4 persons have a very decided individuality, they must not be subjugated by the 1 person, but must be allowed to keep their own distinct character and to see things from their own point of view. If the number 1 person will keep the peculiar temperament of the number 4 in mind, any combination with a number 4 person should be most successful.

Behind all these ideas as far as success is concerned, as I have said at the commencement is the development of the power of concentration *on one's own number*, so as to *increase its influence*. This holds good for all the numbers except those born under the 4 and 8.

In previous chapters I have already warned all those under the 4's and 8's, such as the persons born on the 4th, 8th, 13th, 17th, 22nd, 26th, and 31st to avoid all numbers making an 8 or a 4 as much as possible; not to live in houses that have such numbers, and not to choose dates that make them.

In preceding pages I have gone into fuller details as to the 4 and 8 series, but briefly the rule for such persons to follow is: *Never increase the power of these numbers*. Consequently they must *not* follow the rule laid down for those born under the other numbers, but on the contrary they should do the very opposite.

As they cannot alter their Birth number, they can alter the number made by their name and cause it to produce one of the more fortunate series, especially one of a strong vibration such as a 1, 3, 5, or 6. Having definitely fixed in this way that they are going *to be represented* by the strong number they have made out of their name, they should then follow the rule I gave previously, namely, *think of themselves as that number* and do everything that is important on dates that make that number. If they do this, *and do it persistently*, the number 4 or 8 persons will get away from the bad luck such people generally experience and so become as equally fortunate as others.

They must not, however, expect the change to be seen in a few days, as so many in their impatience do, but in a reasonable space of time they will see very marked results in their favour.

CHAPTER XXVI

MORE INFORMATION ABOUT PERSONS BORN UNDER THE NUMBERS 4 AND 8

I HAVE received so many letters from number 4 and 8 people, asking for advice, that I think it will be useful to devote an entire chapter to such cases.

Out of every hundred letters, fully eighty write testifying to the accuracy of my system of numbers, especially as regards the hard luck that appears to pursue persons who have the combination of 4 and 8 continually cropping up in their lives.

The 4 in itself and all its series is not so much to be dreaded. Persons born on the 4th, 13th, 22nd, and 31st will find these dates and numbers the most important in their lives, but as the 4 in Numerology is always associated with the number 1, and in nearly all systems is written as 4 hyphen 1, or 1 hyphen 4, and as the 1 is a strong and powerful number, I advise the number 4 persons to use *the strong number* as much as possible and select all dates such as the 1st, 10th, 19th, and 28th for their most important efforts, and to endeavour to live in houses whose number or the addition of whose number makes a number 1. They should also remember that as what is called the interchangeable numbers of the 1 hyphen 4 series are the 2 hyphen 7 and all their series, they need not be afraid of such dates or numbers as the 2nd, 6th, 11th, 16th, 20th, 25th or 29th.

It is only when the combination of the 4 and 8 are *continually cropping* up that those born under such numbers should do their utmost to avoid them.

EXAMPLE.—A man born on either the 4th, 13th, 22nd or 31st marries a woman born on either the 8th, 17th, or 26th. He will most certainly find that 4's and 8's will influence his life more than any other number, generally bringing sadness, ill-luck or terrible blows of fate in their train. To this number 4 man or woman, I decidedly say avoid using all 4's and 8's and use the number 1 series instead, and for the next best use the 2 hyphen 7 series.

For some reason, due probably to some law of magnetic vibration, 4 and 8 people generally attract one another, but from *a purely worldly* standpoint the combination cannot be considered "lucky." They often show the highest devotion to one another during illness and misfortune, and some of the greatest examples of self-sacrifice are found when 4's and 8's marry or make a combination together.

Number 8 persons belong to a still more fatalistic law of vibration and appear to be "children of fate" more than any other class.

They can be just as noble in character, as devoted and self-sacrificing as the best of their fellow mortals, but *they seldom get the reward that they are entitled to*. If they rise in life to any high position it is generally one of grave responsibility, anxiety, and care. Such persons can become rich, but wealth seldom brings them happiness, and for love they are generally called on to pay too high a price.

My advice to them is: If they find the 4's and 8's continually coming into their lives and associated with sorrow, disappointment, ill-fate and ill-luck, they should determinately avoid such numbers and all their series. They should, in such a case, so alter their name number, following the examples I have given in previous chapters, to produce one of the more fortunate series, such as 1, 3, 5, or 6, and carry out their plans on dates that make these numbers. If they will do this they will completely alter their ill-luck and control as it were the curious fate that appears to follow them.

If, however, they prefer, as many do, to carry out the *full force and meaning of their number* 8, without caring what the worldly result may be, in that case they should do exactly as I have said for the other numbers and do everything important on dates and numbers that make the 8, such as the 8th, 17th, 26th, also the 4th, 13th, 22nd, and 31st.

If they do this they will be equally successful, but in leading peculiarly fatalistic lives, being, if I may use the expression, "marked" people in whatever path of life they may make their own.

Many have written to ask how to change from an unlucky or fatalistic set of numbers to more fortunate ones. This question is generally asked by people who are born under the series of 4's and 8's, and who have proved, as I have said, that all combinations of such numbers have been more or less associated with fatalistic events in the life. In such cases, when persons are born on the 4th, 13th, 22nd, or 31st in any month they should try to avoid doing important things on dates making the 8 or any of its combinations, such as the 8th, 17th, 26th, and *take instead the number 1 series, or the number of the Zodiacal period of the month they are born in*. For example: A person born between February 19th and March 20th being in the "period of the 3," if they happen to be born on February 22nd or 26th or on March 4th, 8th, 13th, 17th or 22nd, will find it more lucky for them to use the 3 series instead of their birth number, the 4 or 8. In fact, in such cases it will be better for them to drop the birth number altogether.

The same rule will apply to all the other month periods of the year with *the exception of the period* from December 21st to January 20th, the period of the number 8 positive, and from January 21st to February 19th, the period of number 8 negative. If born in these two periods the 4 and 8 people *must not select the number of the month period*, because if they did they would only increase the power of the 4 and 8. I advise them in such cases to take the number of the month period *exactly opposite to their Zodiac period*, which is: For December 21st to January 20th, the opposite numbers are those of June 21st to July 20th, which, if they refer to page 55 of this book, they will find is the period of the 2–7. For people born January 21st to February 19th, the opposite period of the Zodiac is July 31st to August 20th, the numbers of which are 1–4. By following this rule all people who have the 4 and 8 for their birth number will be able to select numbers to use in place of the series of their 4's and 8's, and by employing the new numbers will, in a short time, begin to notice how much more fortunate their lives have become.

They should employ also the colours and jewels which their *new numbers indicate* instead of those given for the 4's and 8's.

I feel sure this information will be useful to many hundreds who have asked questions on this extremely important point.

Many number 2 persons have written and asked me why it is that they find as well as their own number, the 2, 11, 20, and 29th, that the 8 appears to have a great importance in their lives. The reason for this is that the 8, being a very strong number, with a fatalistic tendency, tries to dominate the weaker number 2, which has a relation to itself as 4 times 2 is 8, but the 8 is not a happy combination when it comes into the lives of number 2 persons, and it should always be regarded as a warning of sorrow and disappointment or fatalistic experiences of some kind.

The 4 will also be found to have a great deal of influence with number 2 persons, but this is because it not only represents the double of the number 2, but it is also one of the interchangeable numbers, such as 1 and 4 are the interchangeable numbers of the 2 and 7.

CHAPTER XXVII

THE AFFINITY OF COLOURS AND NUMBERS AND HOW MUSIC AND NUMBERS ARE ASSOCIATED

NUMBER 1 persons, namely those born on the 1st, 10th, 19th, or 28th (numbers which by the addition of themselves produce the number 1), should dress themselves as much as possible in all shades of brown (light or dark) and all shades of yellow or gold colours, or at least have some of these colours about their person. If they have the freedom to select colours for their sleeping rooms, they should follow the same rule.

They will find this colour rule will have an excellent effect in soothing their nerves, and they will rest and sleep better in rooms having their own colours.

Number 2 persons, namely, those born on the 2nd, 11th, 20th, or 29th, should wear all shades of green from the darkest to the lightest shade, also cream and white.

They should avoid all heavy dark colours, especially black, purple, and dark red.

Number 3 persons, namely, those born on the 3rd, 12th, 21st, or 30th, should wear shades of mauve, violet, or the pale or lilac shade of purple, but as men cannot easily dress in such colours, they should at least employ them in their neckties, shirts or handkerchiefs.

Number 4 persons, namely, those born on the 4th, 13th, 22nd, or 31st, should wear what are called the "electric colours," blue, greys, electric blues, and what are known as "half shades." They should avoid strong or positive colours of all kinds.

Number 5 persons, namely, those born on the 5th, 14th, or 23rd, should wear the light shades of all colours, especially light greys, white, and glistening materials.

They should never wear dark colours if they can possibly avoid doing so.

Number 6 persons, namely, those born on the 6th, 15th, or 24th, should wear all shades of blue, from the lightest to the dark navy, what is known as the full or real blue, not "electric blue." For secondary colours, they can also wear shades of rose or pink, but not red, scarlet, or crimson, unless they are born between March 21st to April 24th, or between October 21st to November 24th.

Number 7 persons, namely, those born on the 7th, 16th, or 25th, should, like the number 2 persons wear all shades of pale green, white, yellow, and gold colours. The palest possible shades are best for them, such as what are known as "pastel shades."

Number 8 persons, namely, those born on the 8th, 17th, or 26th, should wear all shades of dark grey, dark blue, purple, and black; light and gaudy colours are out of place with them and should be avoided.

Number 9 persons, namely, those born on the 9th, 18th, or 27th, should wear all shades of red, rose, crimson, pink, or red purple. The darker or rich shades of these colours are best for them.

Red is the colour of the soldier, the colour of energy, restlessness, and revolution. It is the chosen colour of the Revolutionist and Anarchist; hence, the origin of the "red flag."

On account of the magnetic rays sent off by a number 9 person, their presence often irritates people belonging to other numbers, except those born under the number 1, the 3, the 5, the 6, or their own number. People born under the other numbers are very often nervous or uncomfortable in the presence of a number 9 person.

Numbers and music show very decided affinities. The number 1, 3, and 9 persons like martial, inspiring, or what may be called "full-blooded" tones; number 2 and 7 persons are more partial to string and wind instruments, such as the violin, 'cello, harp, pipes, etc.; number 6 persons like romantic, sweet music of all kinds with a lilt and rhythm; number 5 persons lean towards either extremely original or unusual music, something off the beaten track. Number 4 and 8 persons, if musical, have a special leaning for the organ and make magnificent choir or choral leaders, but in all their music there is an undertone of plaintiveness, melancholy, religious fervour or fatalism.

The following are a few examples of countries having their own individual or what is called National Music, in accordance with the planet and number by which they are governed.

England and Germany, governed by Mars (number 9), martial, inspiring, or "full-blooded" music.

Ireland, governed by Venus (number 6), romantic, sweet music, with a lilt or rhythm.

Scotland, governed by the Moon (number 2) and Saturn (number 8), string and wind instruments.

Wales, governed by Uranus (number 4) and Mercury (number 5), original music, with undertone of religious fervour, melancholy, choral, and choir.

The United States, governed by the Planet Mercury (number 5), can use the qualities of that number and adapt itself to all types of music, but will always lean to what is original, new, and out of the ordinary—hence this country is the natural birthplace of what is called "jazz" or syncopated music.

CHAPTER XXVIII

NUMBERS AND DISEASE. PLANETARY SIGNIFICANCE OF HERBAL CURES

IN some of my recent articles in the Press I gave an account of the various diseases that are associated with persons born under the numbers that make their birth date. I have received so many letters testifying to the accuracy of this system and begging me to give further information as to indications from occultism regarding the cure of diseases, that I have much pleasure in giving in this chapter the names of herbs that are beneficial to persons born under the different numbers.

To keep in good health is one of the essentials to success in life, and in following these rules I feel sure my readers can only benefit by this advice.

The same students of occultism who discovered the extraordinary influence of numbers in connection with the destiny of individuals, also discovered the sympathy of certain plants, fruits, and herbs that in the world of nature are related to the planets and months of the year in which people are born, and so evolved a system by which pain and illness can be alleviated by the use of such herbs, or fruits which correspond to each planet and consequently to the number of birth.

I have collected this information from some of the most ancient sources of knowledge on occultism and from those who have devoted their lives to the investigation of the subject. To this I have added my own lifelong experience, in the belief that by the study of nature we may find the secrets of nature and so honour nature's God by fitting in with His purpose and design, which is shown in all things, from the smallest to the greatest.

Number 1 persons, or all those born on the 1st, 10th, 19th, and 28th of any month, have a tendency to suffer from the heart in some form or another, such as palpitation, irregular circulation, and in advanced life, high blood-pressure. They are also likely to have trouble with the eyes, or astigmatism, and would do well to have their sight carefully tested from time to time.

The principal herbs and fruits for number 1 persons, or all those whose birth number is the 1st, 10th, 19th, or 28th, are:

Raisins, camomile, eye-bright, St. John's wort, saffron, cloves, nutmeg, sorrel, borage, gentian root, lavender, bay leaves, oranges, lemons, dates, thyme, myrrh, musk vervain, ginger, barley (barley bread and barley water). Number 1 persons should eat honey as much as possible.

They will find their nineteenth, twenty-eighth, thirty-seventh, and fifty-fifth years will bring them important changes in health one way or the other.

The months to be most guarded against ill-health and overwork are: October, December and January.

Number 2 persons, or all those whose birth number is the 2nd, 11th, 20th, or 29th, have a tendency to suffer with the stomach and digestive organs. They are liable to such things as ptomaine poisoning, gastric troubles, inflammation of the bowels, internal growths, tumours, etc.

The principal herbs for number 2 persons, or those born on the 2nd, 11th, 20th, or 29th of any month, are: Lettuce, cabbages, turnips, cucumber, melon, chicory or endive, rapeseed, colewort, moonwort, linseed, water plantain, and ash of willow.

They will find the twentieth, twenty-fifth, twenth-ninth, forty-third, forty-seventh, fifty-second, and sixty-fifth years will bring them important changes in health. The three months to be most guarded against for ill-health and overwork are January, February, and July.

Number 3 persons, or all those born on the 3rd, 12th, 21st, or 30th, have a tendency to suffer from overstrain of the nervous system, generally brought on by overwork and their desire not to spare themselves in anything they do.

They are inclined to have severe attacks of neuritis and sciatica, also many forms of skin troubles.

The principal herbs for number 3 persons, or those born on the 3rd, 12th, 21st, or 30th of any month, are beets, borage, bilberries, asparagus, dandelion, endive, ewerwort, lungwort, sage, cherries, barberries, strawberries, apples, mulberries, peaches, olives, rhubarb, gooseberries, pomegranates, pineapples, grapes, mint, saffron, nutmegs, cloves, sweet marjoram, St. John's wort, almonds, figs, hazel-nuts, and wheat.

The months to be most guarded against for ill-health and overwork are December, February, June and September. The important years for changes in health are the twelfth, twenty-first, thirty-ninth, forty-eighth, and fifty-seventh.

Number 4 persons, or all those born on the 4th, 13th, 22nd, or 31st, have a likelihood of suffering from mysterious ailments, difficult of ordinary diagnosis. They are more or less inclined to melancholia, and mental disorders, anæmia, pains in the head and back, bladder, and kidneys.

The principal herbs for number 4 persons, or those born on the 4th, 13th, 22nd or 31st of any month, are spinach, sage, pilewort, wintergreen, medlars, iceland-moss, and Solomon's seal. Number 4 persons derive the greatest benefit from electric treatment of all kinds, mental suggestion, and hypnotism. They should be particularly careful to avoid drugs, also highly seasoned dishes and red meat.

The months to be guarded against for ill-health and overwork are January, February, July, August, and September.

The important years for their health, are the thirteenth, twenty-second, thirty-first, fortieth, forty-ninth and fifty-eighth.

Number 5 persons, or all those born on the 5th, 14th, or 23rd, have a tendency to overstrain of the nervous system. They are inclined to attempt too much mentally, to live too much on their nerves. They are likely to bring on such things as neuritis, twitching in the face, eyes, and hands, and are more prone to nervous prostration, insomnia, and paralysis than any other class. Sleep, rest, and quietude are the best medicines they can employ.

The principal herbs for number 5 persons or those born on the 5th, 14th, or 23rd of any month, are carrots, parsnips, sea-kale, oats in the form of oatmeal or bread, parsley, sweet marjoram, champignons, caraway seeds, thyme, nuts of all kinds, but especially hazel-nuts and walnuts.

The months to be most guarded against for ill-health and overwork are June, September, and December.

The important years for changes in their health are the fourteenth, twenty-third, forty-first, and fiftieth years.

Number 6 persons, or all those born on the 6th, or 15th, 24th, are inclined to suffer with the throat, nose, and upper part of the lungs. As a rule they have a strong robust constitution, especially if they can live in the open or in the country, where they can have plenty of air and exercise. Women born under the number 6 often suffer with their breasts and in childbirth are prone to "milk fever." The heart as a general rule becomes affected in the latter years and produces irregular circulation of the blood.

The herbs for number 6 persons, or those born on the 6th, 15th, or 24th of any month, are all kinds of beans, parsnips, spinach, marrows, mint, melons, motherwort, pomegranates, apples, peaches, apricots, figs, walnuts, almonds and the juice of maidenhair-fern, daffodils, wild thyme, musk, violets, vervain, and rose leaves.

The months to be most guarded against for ill-health and overwork are May, October, and November.

They will find that the fifteenth, twenty-fourth, forty-second, fifty-first and sixtieth years will bring them important changes in health.

Number 7 persons, or those who are born on the 7th, 16th, or 25th, are more easily affected by worry and annoyance than any other class. As long as things are going smoothly, they can get through any amount of work, but if worried, either by circumstances or people, they are inclined to imagine things are worse than they are and get easily despondent and melancholy.

They are extremely sensitive to their surroundings; they will gladly accept any responsibility for those who appear to appreciate them; they are unusually conscientious in doing any work that is interesting to them, but as they are stronger mentally than physically, they have often frail bodies that attempt too much for their strength. They are inclined to have some peculiar delicacy in connection with the skin; it is either extremely sensitive to friction, has some peculiarity as regards perspiration, or develops pimples, boils or rashes from anything that disagrees with their digestive organs.

The principal herbs for number 7 persons, or those born on the 7th, 16th, or 25th in any month, are lettuce, cabbage, chicory, or endive, cucumber, colewort, linseed, mushrooms, ceps, sorrel, apples, grapes, and the juices of all fruits. The months to be most guarded against for ill-health and overwork are January, February, July, and August.

The most important years for changes in health are the seventh, sixteenth, twenty-fifth, thirty-fourth, forty-third, fifty-second, and sixty-first.

Number 8 persons, or those born on the 8th, 17th, or 26th, are as a rule more liable to troubles with the liver, bile, intestines, and excretory part of the system than any other class. They are prone to suffer with headaches, diseases of the blood, auto-poisoning, and rheumatism. They should avoid animal food as much as possible and live on fruit, herbs, and vegetables.

The principal herbs for number 8 persons, or those born on the 8th, 17th, or 26th in any month, are spinach, winter green, angelica, wild carrot, marshmallow, plantain, sage, pileworth, ragwort, shepherd's purse, Solomon's seal, vervain, elder flowers, gravel root, mandrake root, celery.

The months to be most guarded against for ill-health and effects of overwork are December, January, February, and July. They will find the most important years for changes in health are the seventeenth, twenty-sixth, thirty-fifth, forty-fourth, fifty-third, and sixty-second.

Number 9 persons, or those born on the 9th, 18th, or 27th, are more or less inclined to fevers of all kinds, measles, smallpox, chicken-pox, scarlatina, and such-like. They should avoid rich food, also alcoholic drinks or wines.

The principal herbs for number 9 persons, or those born

on the 9th, 18th, or 27th of any month, are onions, garlic, leeks, horse-radish, rhubarb, mustard-seed, wormwood, betony, spear-wort, white hellebore, ginger, pepper, broom, rape, madder, hops, danewort, and juice of nettles.

The months to be most guarded against for ill-health or the effects of overwork are April, May, October, and November.

They will find the most important years for changes in the health are the ninth, eighteenth, twenty-seventh, thirty-sixth, forty-fifth, and sixty-third.

The herbs that have been mentioned in these pages can be obtained from all good herbalists in almost all countries. Herbs are nature's own remedies.

CHAPTER XXIX

HOW TO KNOW WHAT CITY, TOWN, OR PLACE IS FORTUNATE FOR ONE TO LIVE IN

IN this chapter I intend to show how each person may more easily find if any city, town, or place is in a harmonious vibration with themselves.

Such information should be of great value to those who find, as so many do, that a certain town or place has proved unfortunate; they may desire to make a change, but as they have nothing to guide them, they do not know what to do or how to arrive at a decision. The following rules will, I believe, be of great help to all such people.

Taking the numbers 1 to 9 as the foundation numbers, which by now all those readers who have followed my books will know are the basic numbers by which all calculation on this earth is founded, I will therefore give examples of how each birth number may be found in any city, town, or place.

Work out the numbers of the name of the city or town by the numbers given to each letter by the Mystic Alphabet which I give on page 70. Put these numbers under each letter and add them together until only one figure remains; if this single number corresponds to the birth number, then the vibrations of that city, town, or place will accord with the individual, and the district indicated by the number should be fortunate for the person whose birth number corresponds with it, and still more so if the person's name number is also in accord.

Number 1 persons, such as all those born on the 1st, 10th, 19th, or 28th, would therefore find the following towns more likely to be favourable. We will take as an example Manchester. The name works out as follows:

MANCHESTER
4 1 5 3 5 5 3 4 5 2 = 37 and 3 plus 7
= 10 or the single number 1.

Other towns that make the number 1 are:

Birmingham	1
Boston	1
New York	1
Alexandria	1
Whitechapel	1

or any other town or place that will by this system produce the number 1.

Number 1 and 4 and number 2 and 7 persons have a greater choice than those born under any of the other numbers, for, as I have previously explained in my writings on this subject, number 1 belongs to the 1 hyphen 4 series whose interchangeable or sympathetic numbers are the 2 hyphen 7 series; therefore number 1, 2, 4 or 7 persons could select all places that give as their single number any of the series of 1, 2, 4, or 7.

Number 2 persons, or all those born on the 2nd, 11th, 20th, or 29th, can select any town whose final number makes any one of the above series, but more especially a town making their own series of the 2. We will take as an example:

$$\text{LEEDS}$$
$$3\ 5\ 5\ 4\ 3 = 20 = 2$$

or any of the following places which all total to the number 2:

Plymouth	2
Los Angeles	2
Norwich	2
Brighton	2

Number 3 persons, or all those born on the 3rd, 12th, 21st, or 30th, can take as an example:

$$\text{CREWE}$$
$$2\ 3\ 5\ 6\ 5 = 21 = 3$$

or any of the following towns which add to the number 3, such as:

Dublin	3
Bath	3
Reading	3
Limerick	3
Moscow	3
Melbourne	3
York	3
Nottingham	3
Devonport	3
Bradford	3

Number 4 persons, or all those born on the 4th, 13th, 22nd, or 31st, can take as an example:

LONDON
3 7 5 4 7 5 = 31 = 4

or any of the following towns which add to the number 4, such as:

Paisley	4
Bristol	4
Leicester	4
Quebec	4
Montreal	4
Stockport	4
Salisbury	4

or any town indicated by the numbers of the 1, 2, 4, or 7 series, as I explained earlier.

Number 5 persons, or all those born on the 5th, 14th, or 23rd, can take as an example:

TAUNTON
4 1 6 5 4 7 5 = 32 = 5

or any of the following towns which add to the number 5, such as:

Southport	. . . . .	5
Portsmouth	. . . . .	5
Chicago	. . . . .	5
Cork	. . . . .	5
Vienna	. . . . .	5

But as the number 5 is the only number that can associate or harmonise with any other number, they need not be so careful as to what place they select, for as they can get on with persons born under any other number almost equally as well as with those born under their own, so in the same way they get on equally well in any city or place no matter what its number may be.

Number 6 persons, or all those born on the 6th, 15th, or 24th, can take as an example:

$$\text{L I V E R P O O L} \\ 3\ 1\ 6\ 5\ 2\ 8\ 7\ 7\ 3 = 42 = 6$$

or any of the following towns, which add to the number 6, such as:

Edinburgh	. . . .	6
Swansea	. . . .	6
Paris	. . . .	6
Dover	. . . .	6
Worthing	. . . .	6
Halifax	. . . .	6
Oxford	. . . .	6
Cologne	. . . .	6
San Francisco	. . .	6
Cowes	. . . .	6
Sheffield	. . . .	6

Number 7 persons, or all those born on the 7th, 16th, or 25th, can take as an example:

$$\text{W I G A N} \\ 6\ 1\ 3\ 1\ 5 = 16 = 7$$

or any of the following towns which add to the number 7, such as:

Doncaster	7
Hollywood	7
Whitehaven	7
Auckland	7
Calcutta	7
Tiverton	7
Grimsby	7
Preston	7

or any town indicated by the numbers of the 1, 2, 4, 7 series, as I explained earlier.

Number 8 persons, or all those born on the 8th, 17th, or 26th, can take as an example:

GLASGOW
3 3 1 3 3 7 6 = 26 = 8

or any of the following towns, such as:

Belfast	8
Stoke-on-Trent	8
Hull	8
Bombay	8
Bournemouth	8

But, as I have explained on page 135 of this book, I advise all number 4 and 8 persons not to increase the influence of the number 8 by employing or living under this strangely fatalistic number, but instead to make their name number work out to a more fortunate vibration, such as those of the 1, 3, 5, or 6 series.

Number 9 persons, or all those born on the 9th, 18th, or 27th, can take as an example:

WOLVERHAMPTON
6 7 3 6 5 2 5 1 4 8 4 7 5 = 63 = 9

or any of the following towns which add to the number 9, such as:

Blackpool	9
Whitehead	9
St. Louis	9

Berlin	.	.	.	.	.	9
Rome	.	.	.	.	.	9
Toronto	.	.	.	.	.	9
Brussels	.	.	.	.	.	9

As I have explained previously, the series of 3, 6, 9, if added together in any direction, produce a 9 as their final digit, so the persons born under any one of these series will find others born under any of these series sympathetic to them, so also can they take any city or town whose final number makes a 3, 6, 9, as if they used only their own individual number.

In conclusion, it should be born in mind that towns and places should be regarded as the *larger octave of harmony*, the number of one's house *the more intimate*, the number of the date and day of the week *the more immediate as regards events*, and the birth number of persons in relation to oneself as *the more personal* as regards our feelings, affections, and home life.

If this is borne in mind, the reason and logic of this special system of Numerology is easily seen, and the harmony it makes for becomes apparent to every student of humanity.

CHAPTER XXX

HORSE-RACING AND NUMBERS

I HAVE received so many letters asking for information as to how my system of numbers could be employed in "betting," that I cannot conclude this book without trying to give some advice on a subject that is of interest to so many thousands.

There is no doubt that the study of numbers can open up a new field for the successful backing of horses, but there is no saying more true than "a little knowledge is a dangerous thing."

My experience is that people are too much inclined to think that because they have proved that the system I teach has such a bearing on the leading events in their own individual lives, that without more preparation they are ready to plunge into racing and back any horse whose name makes the same number as their own.

The point so many people seem to forget is that horse-racing is an extremely complicated business, so much so that "tips," even from owners and jockeys, are as a rule as equally unreliable as the hundred and one systems that are offered daily to the public by almost every newspaper that one picks up.

Many important racing events have upset all theories as to forecasting the winner by a study of "form," previous running, and so forth. At many races complete outsiders have, for no apparent reason, beaten the most heavily backed favourites.

Can the study of numbers be used to give a clear indication of which horses are likely to be first, second, and third?

I say most emphatically that it can, but the trouble is that it is so rare to find persons who can "keep their heads" when it comes to such a thing as a *systematic employment of any method*, and more particularly with numbers.

If one really made up one's mind to experiment with the

system of numbers as set out in these pages in connection with betting, one would have to do it on the following lines:

To attend the race meeting in person.

Select a day whose number accords with one's own.

If possible, find out the jockeys whose birth number is the same as the number of the day.

When all these numbers are in accord, say, for example, if they all worked out to a number, such as the 9, then such horses, if they run under the numbers 9, 18, and 27 on that day would certainly be more likely to come in as first, second, and third than any others.

In such a case it would be necessary to back the three horses that are to run under the numbers 9, 18, and 27 on the starting board for "win and place." If there were a greater number than 36 running in the race it would be necessary also to take in the horse under that number, but if too much money would be at stake by backing all four, a good rule is to select *the two youngest horses* out of the four and back these two for "win and place." If there were not much difference in age, the next rule to employ is to select *the youngest male horse* in preference to *the youngest female*. If on the first race, one lost on the following race the stakes should be doubled, and so on systematically during the day. If this plan were carried out and the numbers selected steadfastly adhered to, one would sooner or later be rewarded by a first, second, or it may be all three, with the added chance of getting a complete outsider in some of the events.

The great difficulty is that so few persons at a race meeting have sufficient strength of will to follow such a plan systematically. They may try it for one race and, because they have not met with immediate success, they are likely to do nothing for the next event or plunge after some "tip" they have had given them, and so on.

To those who are unable to attend the race meeting personally, I do not advise them to try to "find the winner" by numbers, for the simple reason that if they have not got *the running number of the horse* they miss one of the principal elements for success.

CHAPTER XXXI

EXAMPLES FROM THE NAMES OF SOME PRESIDENTS OF THE UNITED STATES

GEORGE WASHINGTON

IN taking illustrations from the names of Presidents of the United States, I cannot do better than start with the name of George Washington.

```
GEORGE   WASHINGTON
3 5 7 2 3 5   6 1 3 5 1 5 3 4 7 5
  2 5                     4 0
  ───                     ───
   7                       4 = 11 = 2
```

The number of the famous name of George Washington, the 1st President of the United States, worked out by the Chaldean or Hebrew alphabet, as set out in the article on Lloyd George, gives to the name GEORGE the compound number of 25, with its single or final digit of 7. On looking up the meaning of the compound number of 25 on page 83, it will be found stated:

This is a number denoting strength gained through experience and benefits obtained through observation of people and things. It is not deemed exactly "lucky," as its success is given through strife and trials in the earlier life. It is favourable when it appears in regard to the future.

The word WASHINGTON works out to the compound number of 40, with its single digit of 4.

The meaning of this compound number is given on page 84 as:

This is a number of thoughtful deduction, retrospection and mental superiority over one's fellows, but as it seems to belong to the mental plane, the persons it represents are likely to put all material things on one side—not because they have to, but because they wish to do so.

This is remarkably borne out by Washington's resignation of the position of Commander-in-Chief of the victorious American Army when he met his assembled Generals for the last time. His own words were, "With heart full of love and gratitude, I now take leave of you." Addressing the President of Congress, Washington said:

The great events on which my resignation depended having, at length, taken place, I have now the honour to surrender into their [Congress's] hands the trust committed to me and to claim the indulgence of retiring from the service of my country. Having now finished the work assigned me, I retire.

This really great man, so justly called the "Father of the United States," refused to accept any reward for his long years of arduous service, and thus retired to his home at Mount Vernon.

The distinguished name of George Washington bears out in a remarkable manner the occult meaning of the numbers of this name.

If the final digits of 7 for GEORGE and 4 for WASHINGTON be added together they produce eleven (11), with the single digit of 2. This compound number 11, on being raised to its higher octave, 20, gives for this compound number (see page 82) the symbol of "The Awakening," also "The Judgment," with the interpretation,

The awakening of new purpose, new plans, new ambitions, the call to action, but for some great purpose, cause, or duty.

It will thus be seen from this example how wonderfully this system of Numerology fits in with and explains the underlying qualities of the character of George Washington.

By knowing the birth date of an individual and seeing if the number of the date is in harmonious vibration with the number given by the name is of considerable help in arriving at a summing up of the general characteristics.

If the number of the birth date and the number given by the name are not in accord, the promise of the man's or woman's career will not be so definite.

Returning to the name of George Washington, as an example, the last digit is the figure 2, with 7 and 4 as the principal digits of the name.

Now, Washington's birthday is celebrated as February 22nd, which makes the double figure in this system to be written as 4 hyphen 1, with its interchangeable numbers of 2 hyphen 7. (See page 46.) Some people claim that his birth date was February 11th, in the old-style calendar. Should this be the date taken, it would not alter the effect of the number of his name working out to the final digit of a 2, because, whether it was February 22nd, a 4, or February 11th, a 2, they are both interchangeable numbers with one another, and in consequence the number of the name and the number of the birth date *are in harmonious vibration together*.

Should the number of the name and the number of the birth date not be in harmony or accord, it indicates that one is likely to find a jumble or unevenness in the plans and careers of the man or woman the numbers not in vibration to one another represent.

ABRAHAM LINCOLN

Abraham Lincoln born February 12, 1809, assassinated on the night of Friday, April 14, 1865, died April 15.

The name works out as follows:

```
A B R A H A M   L I N C O L N
1 2 2 1 5 1 4   3 1 5 3 7 3 5
  ─────────     ─────────────
     1 6              2 7
     ───              ───
      7                9      = 16 = 7
```

In this case the birth number, the single digit 3, and the single digit of the name are not in harmonious accord.

The single digit of 3 for the birth is a powerful number, being in itself representative of the Planet Jupiter; it indicates underlying ambition, the power to rule and dictate. In describing these persons on page 43, I have stated:

Number 3 people . . . are decidedly ambitious; they are never satisfied in being in subordinate positions; their aim is to rise in the world, to have control and authority over others. They are excellent in the execution of commands; they love order and discipline in all things; they readily obey orders themselves, but they also insist on having their orders obeyed. Number 3 people often rise to the very highest positions in any business, profession, or sphere in which they may be found. They often excel in position of authority in the Army and Navy, in Government, and in life generally; and especially in all posts of trust and responsibility, as they are extremely conscientious in carrying out their duties.

The final digit of the name ABRAHAM LINCOLN, a 7, is more weak or gentle in its qualities, as I have stated on page 55:

People born under the number 7 . . . are very independent, original, and have strongly marked individuality . . . but in everything they do, they sooner or later show a peculiar philosophical outlook on life that tinges all their work.

On page 56, I further said, number 7 people have "a peculiar magnetism that has great influence over others."

The description by this system of Numerology, it must be admitted, accords closely with the well-known character of Abraham Lincoln.

Turning to the more mysterious or hidden influences indicated by the compound numbers, if we add the single digit of the birth number, the 3, to the digit of the name number, the 7, they produce the compound number of 10. On page 80 we read:

10. Symbolised as the "Wheel of Fortune." It is a number of honour, of faith and self-confidence, of rise and fall; one's name will be known for good or evil, according to one's desires;

it is a fortunate number in the sense that one's plans are likely to be carried out.

Taking the compound number of the birth, February 12th, for another indication of the occult influences governing this career, we read for this number on page 80:

12. The symbolism of this number is suffering and anxiety of mind. It is also indicated as "the Sacrifice" or "the Victim" and generally foreshadows one being sacrificed for the plans or intrigues of others.

Now, turning to the compound number of the name, 16, we read on page 81:

16. This number has a most peculiar occult symbolism. It is pictured by "a Tower Struck by Lightning from which a man is falling with a Crown on his head." It is also called "the Shattered Citadel."
It gives warning of some strange fatality awaiting one.

When one considers Lincoln's sudden assassination as he sat in a box in a theatre on the night of Friday, April 14th, one cannot help being astonished at the truth underlying this system of occult significance of the compound numbers.
Further, Abraham Lincoln was the 16th President of the United States, the single digit of this number, the 7, corresponding to the single digit of his name.

GROVER CLEVELAND

Grover Cleveland, 22nd President of the United States, born March 18th, 1837, died June 24th, 1908.
The numbers that are formed by the name of Grover Cleveland are as follows:

```
G R O V E R   C L E V E L A N D
3 2 7 6 5 2   3 3 5 6 5 3 1 5 4
─────────     ─────────────────
   2 5             3 5
   ───             ───
    7               8         = 15 = 6
```

The birth number, March 18th, gives the single digit of 9. If one will refer back to the illustration on page 31, one will also see that this date fell into the period of the number 3 (Negative) or House of Jupiter, the planet whose number is a 3.

The addition of all the figures made by the name GROVER CLEVELAND works out to the single digit of 6. Even his death, which took place on June 24th, came on a date whose figures, by addition, 2 plus 4, made a 6, and the year in which he died, 1908, which, if added together, produced, for its last digit, the 9; the same as the day of birth, which also made the figure of 9.

Here we have a remarkable example of the birth and name number being in accord, as the numbers of 3, 6, 9 are interchangeable and in harmonious vibration with one another.

On my visit to Washington during the Cleveland Administration, both the President and Mrs. Cleveland received me in a most hospitable way. One afternoon, while having tea with the Lady of the White House, the President dropped in at the end of a Cabinet meeting, and, seeing me engaged in reading Mrs. Cleveland's hands and working out her fadic numbers, he became interested and had me work out his own.

He was especially struck by the curious predominance of the numbers 3, 6, 9, and all their series that appeared to run like milestones through his life.

The compound number of his name, namely 15, if the reader will turn back to page 80, he will find described as:

. . . a number of occult significance, of magic and mystery; but as a rule it does not represent the higher side of occultism, its meaning being that the persons represented by it will use every art of magic they can to carry out their purpose. If associated with a good or fortunate single number, it can be very lucky and powerful.

(This was so in Grover Cleveland's case; the last digit of his birth number being a 9, the number of Mars, a strong number in his combination.)

To continue the description of the compound Number 15, as set out on page 81, it goes on to say:

It is peculiarly associated with "good talkers," often with eloquence, gifts of Music and Art and a dramatic personality, combined with voluptuousness and strong personal magnetism.

This description of what may be called "the inner side," which the compound number of a name always denotes, was peculiarly suitable to the well-known character of Grover Cleveland.

WARREN G. HARDING

Warren G. Harding, 29th President of the United States, was born at Blooming Grove, Ohio, on November 2nd, 1865. Died August 3rd, 1923, of some form of poisoning, supposed to be ptomaine. His sudden death on the eve of an investigation into his administration caused a considerable amount of sensation and speculation.

The numbers of his name are as follows:

```
W A R R E N    G    H A R D I N G
6 1 2 2 5 5    3    5 1 2 4 1 5 3
  2 1                  2 1

    3          3         3     = 9
```

Here we have an example of *no accord or harmonious vibration* between the birth number, November 2nd, and the number of the name, whose final digit is 9.

The 2 (as I stated on page 40) "stands in symbolism for the Moon," while the 9 "stands in symbolism for the Planet Mars" (see page 64). Consequently, in this case, there is a complete dissimilarity and disaccord in the qualities expressed by these numbers.

In a previous chapter I have explained that when the birth number and name number are not in accord, considerable jumble or unevenness may be expected in the person's career. In the case under observation, one could hardly find a greater dissimilarity than in the qualities expressed by the numbers of the Moon (2) and Mars (9). Had President Harding lived for even another year, there is no doubt that great irregularities would have been brought to light in connection with his term of office.

As no compound number was made by the birth date, November 2nd, or by the letters of the name, which came to a 9, to find a compound number we must, therefore, add the name number and birth number together, 9 plus 2 equals 11. Turning back to the explanation given to compound numbers (on page 80) for the number 11, we read:

This is an ominous number to occultists. It gives warning of hidden dangers, trial, and treachery from others. It has a symbol of "a Clenched Hand" and "a Lion Muzzled."

The symbolism in this case is still more emphasised by the fact that the birth number and the name number are, as I have explained in a preceding paragraph, in extreme disaccord, indicating general muddle and *want of harmony in the affairs of life*.

This example is the exact opposite of the illustration I have given of the numbers governing the destiny of Calvin Coolidge, whose numbers, the 4 and 7, are *interchangeable* and *in harmony with one another*. So that, though by addition they produce the number 11 and give the same symbol, it is not the "Clenched Hand" and the "Lion Muzzled" by fear, as in President Harding's case; but the harmonious control of self that, in such a position of responsibility, surrounded by "hidden dangers, trial, and treachery from others" required to be "a Clenched Hand" and "a Lion Muzzled" in order to escape.

Returning to Warren G. Harding, by a curious coincidence, he was in his fifty-seventh year leading up to his mysterious death on August 3rd, 1923. The number 57 added together produces the compound number 12. This is described on page 80 as follows:

The symbolism of this number is suffering and anxiety of mind. It is also indicated as "the Sacrifice" or "the Victim" and generally foreshadows one being sacrificed for the plans or intrigues of others.

To anyone who has read the history of President Harding's career, this is, alas! a fitting description of the last year of his life.

THEODORE ROOSEVELT

Theodore Roosevelt, the 26th President of the United States, was born October 27th, 1858. Died January 6th, 1919.

The numbers of his name are as follows:

$$\begin{array}{cc} \text{THEODORE} & \text{ROOSEVELT} \\ 4\,5\,5\,7\,4\,7\,2\,5 & 2\,7\,7\,3\,5\,6\,5\,3\,4 \\ \hline 3\,9 = 1\,2 & 4\,2 \\ \hline 3 & 6 \quad = 9 \end{array}$$

The single digit of the birth number, October 27th, gives not only the Mars number of 9, but (if one refers back to the illustration on page 31) one will see that this part of October, in the Zodiac, is placed in the period of number 9 (Negative), also called the House of Mars.

Theodore Roosevelt was, therefore, *by both birth number and name number*, a Mars man in the truest sense of the word. He was a born fighter; independent in spirit, he cared nothing for the opinions of others.

He was put into the position of Vice-President of the United States in order to prevent his becoming President. Fate had, however, ordained otherwise; the assassination of William McKinley on October 14th, 1901, placed him in the highest office of the American nation.

Mars men, if they rise to any important position, rarely escape attempts against their lives. Theodore Roosevelt was no exception to this rule. On October 14th, 1912, he was badly wounded in an anarchist's attempt to assassinate him.

If one reads the description of number 9 persons which I have given (in Chapter XI), it would appear to have been written to fit his case:

Number 9 persons are fighters in all they attempt in life. They usually have difficult times in their early years, but generally they are, in the end, successful by their grit, strong will, and determination.

In character, they are hasty in temper, impulsive, independent and desire to be their own masters.

When the Number 9 is noticed to be more than usually dominant in the dates and events of their lives, they will be found to make great enemies, to cause strife and opposition wherever they may be, and they are often wounded or killed either in warfare or in the battle of life.

They have great courage and make excellent soldiers or leaders in any cause they espouse.

As there is no compound number in the digits of the name THEODORE ROOSEVELT, one obtains it by the addition of the 9 of the name number to the 9 of the birth number, 9 plus 9 equals 18. Looking up this compound number (on page 81), one reads:

It is symbolic of materialism striving to destroy the spiritual side of the nature. It generally associates a person with bitter quarrels, even family ones, also with war, revolutions, social upheavals; and in some cases it indicates making money and position through wars or by wars.

Theodore Roosevelt may not have made money out of the Spanish-American War, but he certainly did make position, for, as organiser and commander of Roosevelt's Rough Riders, his name became a household word, not only in the United States, but in the world itself.

I had the honour of meeting this really great man on two occasions when he was Governor of New York State. He was frank enough and materialistic enough to tell me he did not believe in occultism in any form, and yet, after the death of Major John A. Logan, which I had predicted several years in advance, as related in my *Memoirs*,[1] he admitted that this occurrence had compelled him to alter his views on the mysterious workings of Fate.

WOODROW WILSON

Woodrow Wilson, 28th President of the United States, was born December 28th, 1856. Died February 3rd, 1924.

The numbers of his name are as follows:

$$\begin{array}{cc} \text{WOODROW} & \text{WILSON} \\ 6\ 7\ 7\ 4\ 2\ 7\ 6 & 6\ 1\ 3\ 3\ 7\ 5 \\ \hline 3\ 9 = 12 & 2\ 5 \\ \hline 3 & 7 = 10 = 1 \end{array}$$

The single digit of his birth number is 28=10 or 1, as the zero does not count. The single digit of his name works out to a 1. 28th President, the final digit is also a 1. This is a remarkable example of harmonious vibration between the birth number and name number.

In writing of number 1 persons (on page 38), I have explained that, in this system of Numerology, the number 1 is always written as the figure 1 hyphen 4 and its interchangeable numbers as 2 hyphen 7.

These numbers were intimately associated with the most important acts of President Wilson's life, as any person will observe who looks up his career:

Born December 28th	Produces a 1
The year 1856	,, ,, 2
Year of death, 1924	,, ,, 7
28th President	,, ,, 1
Last digit of name	,, ,, 1
Inaugurated President 1st time March 4th	,, ,, 4

[1] *Confessions: Memoirs of a Modern Seer*, Jarrold's Ltd., London.

His note to Germany on *Lusitania*, May 13th . Produces a 4
Severed diplomatic relations with Germany,
February 4th . . . . ,, ,, 4
Took oath of office 2nd time March 4th . . ,, ,, 4
His War message to Congress, April 2nd . . ,, ,, 2
Landed in France, December 13th . . . ,, ,, 4
First convoy of ships to Great War, June 13th . ,, ,, 4
Decisive battle U.S. troops at St. Mihiel, September 13th . . . . ,, ,, 4
Armistice signed, November 11th . . . ,, ,, 2

The compound number of 10 made by his name (as set out on page 80) reads:

Symbolised as the "Wheel of Fortune." It is a number of honour, of faith and self-confidence, of rise and fall; one's name will be known for good or evil, according to one's desires; it is a fortunate number in the sense that one's plans are likely to be carried out.

Whether the Senate and Congress disagreed with President Wilson or not, one must admit that he carried through his famous "Fourteen Points" at the Treaty of Versailles.

CALVIN COOLIDGE

Calvin Coolidge, 30th President of the United States, was born in the state of Vermont on July 4th, 1872.

The numbers made by his name are as follows:

```
C A L V I N   C O O L I D G E
3 1 3 6 1 5   3 7 7 3 1 4 3 5
─────────     ─────────────
 1 9 = 1 0      3 3
 ───            ─────
   1            6 = 7
```

As there is no compound number produced by the letters of this name, we must add the birth number of the 4 to the single digit of the name, the 7, thus producing the compound number of 11. On page 80 we read:

> This is an ominous number to occultists. It gives warning of hidden dangers, trial, and treachery from others. It has a symbol of "a Clenched Hand" and "a Lion Muzzled."

This may account for the proverbial reticence, silence, and noncommittal utterances of a man who, from small beginnings, rose to be President of the United States.

The fact that the name number 7 is one of the interchangeable numbers with the 4 of the birth date, placed these numbers *in harmonious vibration with one another*, which, no doubt, was a considerable factor in the success of his remarkable career.

Calvin Coolidge, having the number 4 for his birth number, especially in the period of the year of the 2 hyphen 7 (as will be seen if one turns back to page 46), was not a worldly man or one craving for power. It was, consequently, extremely difficult for him to come out of his retirement and stand again for President unless some unusual influence had been brought to bear on his decision not to do so.

His numbers indicate him to be of an extremely sensitive nature, one not caring for the clash and turmoil of political strife. Nothing short of a great national crisis in the affairs of his country, or a unanimous demand from the people, would, in my opinion, have influenced such a man to face again a Presidential campaign.

In passing, I may remark that during his term as President he sent me a letter of appreciation on my book, *Cheiro's World Predictions*.

Ex-President Calvin Coolidge died January 5th, 1933.

HERBERT HOOVER

Herbert Hoover, 31st President of the United States, was born August 10th, 1874.

In his early years he wrote his name as Herbert Clark Hoover, which produced the following numbers:

HERBERT CLARK HOOVER
5 5 2 2 5 2 4 3 3 1 2 2 5 7 7 6 5 2

2 5	1 1	3 2
7	2	5 ≡ 14 ≡ 5

Later on in life he dropped the word CLARK in general use and became universally known as:

HERBERT HOOVER
5 5 2 2 5 2 4 5 7 7 6 5 2

2 5	3 2
7	+ 5 = 12 = 3

His birth number is 1 hyphen 4, with the interchangeable numbers of 2 hyphen 7, which are all the more dominant for the reason that he was born in that part of the Zodiac known as the period of the 1–4 positive (see illustration, page 31). If his birth number is written out, the importance of these numbers will be quickly observed as:

$$\left.\begin{array}{l}\text{10th} = 1\text{–}4\\ \text{August} = 1\text{–}4\\ 1874\,(20) = 2\text{–}7\end{array}\right\}\!-\!8$$

As the opposite Sign of the Zodiac is January, the House of Saturn (Positive), the 8 representing this planet should be placed in opposition, like the above example. The above illustration denotes, at a glance, how dominant the 1–4 of the birth number is in this case.

The name number, which works out to the single digit of 3, although the strong number of Jupiter, becomes, in this case, a secondary number.

It would have been better (as I have explained in previous illustrations) if the name number worked out to a similar combination as that of the birth. If it had, it would cause a more harmonious vibration and less of a jumble in his affairs in later years.

From the preceding example of the birth number, it will be seen that Herbert Hoover is decidedly a number 1 man. Writing on this number (on page 37), I have stated:

. . . a person born under the Birth number of 1, or any of its series, has the underlying principles of being in his or her work, creative, inventive, strongly individual, definite in his or her views, and in consequence more or less obstinate and determined in all they as individuals undertake. This relates to all men and women born under the number 1, such as on the 1st, 10th, 19th, or 28th of any month (the addition of all these numbers making a 1), but *more especially so* if they happen to be born between the 21st July to the 28th August, which is the period of the Zodiac called the "House of the Sun." . . .

Number 1 people are ambitious; they dislike restraint, they always rise in whatever their profession or occupation may be. They desire to become the heads of whatever their businesses are, and as departmental chiefs they keep their authority and make themselves respected and "looked up to" by their subordinates.

This, I think, will be admitted by all impartial observers to be a description fitting in well with the career of a man who from very ordinary beginnings rose to be President of one of the greatest nations of the world.

Looking back over some of the important phases of Herbert Hoover's career, the numbers 1–4 stand out very clearly. At the age of 19, which works out to the single digit of 1, he got his first appointment with the U.S.A. Geological Survey. This was the foundation for his being called to Australia to take charge of the famous Coolgardie gold-mines. From this his company appointed him manager of a mine they purchased, called the "Sons of Gwalia," which he built up to become one of the best-paying properties in the West Australian field.

From here he went to China, where he discovered the world's largest coal deposits underlying the north-eastern province.

During the Boxer revolution he was called on to play an important role in organising the defence of Tientsin, which, later, brought him into close contact with the representatives of European nations who had sent troops to protect their nationals.

In 1900, again a 1-4 number, he was called on to reorganise the great Chinese Company with its 25,000 workers at Tong Shan, which, under his management, showed profits for the first time in its history.

It was, however, the 1914-1918 War that gave Herbert Hoover his greatest opportunity. On November 13th (a 4-1 number), 1914, he got his first food ship into Rotterdam, and the starving population of Belgium were saved. By the end of the war he had raised the sum of $4,000,000 for the help of this country alone, and when the books of his relief organisation were closed, the auditors certified that its sales and purchase account was the huge total of $928,000,000. It is significant that they added a statement to their report that "Herbert Hoover had never, himself, drawn a cent from these funds for travelling expenses or for any other purpose whatever."

On March 4th, 1921, he entered President Wilson's Administration in the quite humble position of Secretary of Commerce. From this position he rose in 1929 to become President of the United States, being elected by a greater majority of votes than any other man who had, up to then, reached the Presidential chair.

It is a curious coincidence that President Hoover filled this exalted position as the 31st President, a number in itself making a 4.

If readers will turn back to my previous remarks on the apparently fatalistic importance of the numbers of 4's and 8's, they will realise what a vital meaning may be attached to the fact that President Hoover is a 1-4 man with the number 8 in Zodiacal opposition.

On page 84 one may read that in occult symbolism, the number 31 is "not a fortunate number from a worldly or material standpoint."

In many ways it must be admitted that the United States, under its 31st President, in spite of all his great powers of organisation, had not been fortunate "from a worldly or material standpoint." Unemployment had risen to the highest figure in history; Stock Exchange panics had ruined or impoverished millions of people. Standard shares like U.S. steel fell to the lowest levels conceivable, while universal trade depression sapped the foundations of Industry.

Under its 31st President, the United States was faced by a greater problem of Prohibition than ever before. Large revenue had been lost, money had been diverted into the hands of "gangsters" and outlaws, and crime stalked brazenly through the land.

In the middle of this critical and dangerous situation, the 31st President conceived the idea of giving a moratorium of a year to the debtor-nations of the United States.

In his generous effort to help broken-down European nations, I fear President Hoover's gift only augmented their squabbles and resulted in his own "crucification," as has happened to other "Saviours" who have attempted to help ungrateful humanity.

Those born about the centre of the month of August often rise to great positions, but as often suffer equally great reverses. History gives us many examples: Napoleon, born August 15th; Louis XVI, born August 23rd; the Emperor Francis Joseph of Austria, born August 18th; Empress Elizabeth of Austria (assassinated), born August 18th,; the Czarevitch, born August 9th; President Carnot of France (assassinated), born August 11th.

FRANKLIN DELANO ROOSEVELT

Franklin Delano Roosevelt, the 32nd President of the United States, was born at Hyde Park, New York, at 8.18 p.m., January 30th, 1882.

The numbers made by his name are as follows:

```
F R A N K L I N   D E L A N O   R O O S E V E L T
8 2 1 5 2 3 1 5   4 5 3 1 5 7   2 7 7 3 5 6 5 3 4
-----------       ---------     -----------------
    2 7              2 5              4 2
    ---              ---              ---
     9                7              6 = 22 = 4
```

CHEIRO'S BOOK OF NUMBERS 171

It will be noticed that his birth date, January 30th, produces for its single digit the powerful number of 3, which my readers will remember earlier in this book stands for the planet Jupiter.

The power of the number 3 is, in his case, however, afflicted, especially through his early years, by its being in the period of the planet Saturn, the 8 negative.

The qualities of persons born in this Zodiacal Sign of Aquarius I have described in my book, *When Were You Born?*[1] The foundation indications are as follows:

Persons born in this part of the Zodiac are generally very active for the public good and will often give all they have to relieve the distress of others. They are good reasoners, and are very successful in debate and argument and difficult to convince.

They are excellent in business and finance when they apply their minds to such things, but as a general rule they are more successful for others than for themselves.

They take a great interest in public meetings, large gatherings of people and public ceremonies.

They have a quiet controlling power with their eyes, and so subdue others. It takes some sudden call of circumstances to make them "make the most of themselves."

In matters of health they are inclined to suffer from the nerves of the stomach in some peculiar manner that is difficult to relieve by ordinary medicine. They are prone to suffer from accidents to their teeth, pains in the knees and feet and trouble *with the middle of the spine.*

Franklin Delano Roosevelt, however, being born under the powerful number of the 3, the indicator of strong will, determination and ambition, was able to rise above the indications given by his Zodiacal Sign, even to conquer the spinal meningitis which attacked him in his early days.

In previous pages of this book describing the qualities of number 3 persons, I have stated:

Number 3 people, like the number 1 individuals, are decidedly ambitious; they are never satisfied by being in subordinate

---

[1] Published by Herbert Jenkins, Ltd., 3 Duke of York Street, Saint James's, London.

positions; their aim is to rise in the world, *to have control and authority over others.*

Number 3 people often rise to the very highest positions in any business, profession or sphere in which they may be found. They often excel in positions of authority in the army and navy, in government and in life generally; and especially in all posts of trust and responsibility, as they are extremely conscientious in carrying out their duties.

This appears to be a very fitting description of the 32nd President of the United States.

When we come to analyse the birth and name number, we find, however, they are not in harmony with one another.

The birth date, January 30th, is a 3, while the name number works out to a 22, or the single digit of a 4.

In dealing with the numbers governing President Harding, I called attention to the fact that "when the birth number and name number are not in accord, considerable jumble or unevenness may be expected in the person's career." There is, however, a very considerable divergency when one examines closely the other numbers associated with these two men's lives.

President Harding was the 29th President. This compound number, as I have stated, "indicates uncertainties, treachery and deception of others."

President Roosevelt, being the 32nd President on the contrary comes, as Head of his Nation, under a fortunate compound number, *at least as far as his country is concerned.* In dealing with the number 32, I have stated in previous pages of this book (page 84):

This number has a magical power. It is usually associated with combinations of people or nations. It is a fortunate number if the person it represents holds to his own judgment or opinions; if not, his plans are likely to become wrecked by the stubbornness and stupidity of others. It is a favourable number if it appears in connection with future events.

The compound number of President Roosevelt's name, which works out to a 22, is, however, not so fortunate *personally.* I have stated in earlier pages:

CHEIRO'S BOOK OF NUMBERS

This number is symbolised by "a good man blinded by the folly of others, with a knapsack on his back full of errors."

It is a warning number of illusion and delusion, a good person who lives in a fool's paradise; a dreamer of dreams who awakens only when surrounded by danger. It is also a number of false judgment *owing to the influence of others*.

President Roosevelt ran considerable danger of assassination in the course of his career. The indications were very similar to those given in the life of Abraham Lincoln, whose birth number was also a 3 in the Zodiacal Sign of Aquarius in the House of Saturn, the negative number 8.

President Roosevelt had a close call from death, when Zangara, the anarchist, fired six shots at him on February 15th, 1933, at Miami, Florida, and Mayor Cermak of Chicago was fatally wounded by his side.

NOTE.—The title of President is not taken into account in this system of Numerology, as is that of Kings, Queens, hereditary titles, or those given for life. The reason being that the title of President is only for a term of years and is therefore a transitory one.

CHAPTER XXXII

THE BIBLE AND NUMBERS

IN the opening chapters of this book, I have given illustrations of the influence of the number 7 and other numbers in connection with the Hebrew race.

In my more recent book, *Cheiro's World Predictions*, I have gone more fully into an explanation of why the Twelve Tribes were called "the chosen people," and why their destiny has affected more races on the earth than any other.

One of the great wonders of the world has been the fact that, in spite of privations and persecutions such as no other race ever endured, the Jewish people have held to their religion as set out in the pages of the volume of the Sacred Law, and furthermore, that this volume has become *the base of all law in every land and clime into which it has permeated*.

It is acknowledged to have the greatest influence for good of any book that has ever been written. It is considered the inspired message of God the Creator to the Hebrew race in the first instance, and later to all mankind.

In this book, generally called the Bible, more knowledge is at times concealed than is revealed to the ordinary reader.

Like a mine, its purest gold may not be found on the surface; its richest veins may only reward those who have the patience to toil for years, whose lamp of faith, no matter how dim at times, keeps steadily burning—until somehow or somewhere, the thread of gold is found that leads upwards and onwards even to the Creator Himself.

It would be rank presumption on my part if I made an attempt to elucidate even a fraction of those wonders of the Sacred Volume that are revealed to some and concealed from others.

Such an account of these revelations may perhaps be better left in the hands of those whose profession or ministry gives them more intimate cause to interpret its meanings in support of whatever creed or religion they represent.

For me, it will be sufficient in the short space at my disposal if I am able to call attention to one single instance—but one of radiant importance—to prove that this wonderful book not only has in its pages the evidence of Divine Design in the Creator's construction of things—but that *it contains in itself a systematic plan and design* that must carry with it incontrovertible proof that not only is the Sacred Volume inspired, but that it has within itself *the proofs of its inspiration*, so that all mankind might believe in its message.

It has been handed down to us that the first books of the Bible were written or compiled by one of the greatest men of all time, a man called Moses.

Let us consider for a moment who this man was and what his claims are for universal respect and admiration. Briefly, he was born of the priestly house of Levi. He was called Moses because Pharaoh's daughter saved him from the waters of the Nile. He was adopted by her *and became her son*.

In this position, as the child of the great Pharaoh's daughter, he received the highest education that was possible in that wonderful land of Egypt. The Sacred Book tells us "he was versed in all the wisdom of the Egyptians." History tells us that he became a Master of Astrology, that he erected a great observatory in the Temple of the Sun at Heliopolis.

When his supposed mother became Queen of Egypt, Moses became commander-in-chief of her army; as such he conquered the Ethiopians and relieved Egypt from danger of invasion.

In this moment of triumph the Queen died, a Pharaoh came to the throne who "knew not Moses," and the Bible says, "he went out unto his brethren and looked on their burdens." The "call of the blood" had come; he knew he was a Hebrew, the son of the priestly tribe of Levi;

"he saw an Egyptian smiting one of his brethren"[1]; he slew the Egyptian and took refuge in the land of Midian.

Moses was now eighty years of age,[2] a man of experience, a man accustomed to responsibility and power, a man of great learning, "versed in all the wisdom of the Egyptians." Such was the man the Lord had chosen for the delivery of His people.

I will pass over the message from "the burning bush," that command that has passed down through the ages: "I AM that I AM."

I must leave to the imagination of my readers the humbling of Pharaoh by the ten plagues, the passover night, the outward march of that multitude of men, women, and herds of cattle. No one but Moses, who had been a commander-in-chief, could have organised such a march.

What a milestone in history—the first passover of the Hebrews as a nation. What a meaning it must have had for a people in slavery.

The end of four hundred and thirty years of bondage to the Egyptians, "that night of the Lord to be observed of all the children of Israel in their generation."[3]

The first great passover of the Hebrews took place at the full moon after the Spring Equinox in the first month of the Hebraic year, the month which is called Abib.

If one looks at an atlas containing the old Hebrew names, it is easy to see that Moses skilfully led this great multitude of people towards the most fordable part of the Red Sea at the northern end of the Gulf of Suez, at a place called Pi-hahiroth, as stated in the Bible.[4]

Moses was well acquainted with this part of the country, having passed this way on his flight to Midian and his return to Egypt. He had observed the influx of the tides, and by his astrological calculations he knew that the southeastern monsoon would arrive at a certain date to aid his plans. This is the east wind mentioned in the English version of the Bible; in the Septuagint, it is called a strong southern wind; but in both the poetical description is the

---

[1] Exodus ii. 11.
[2] Ibid., vii. 7.
[3] Exodus xii. 42.
[4] Ibid., xiv. 2.

same, "and the Lord caused the sea to go back by a strong east wind all that night and made the sea dry land and the waters were divided"[1] . . . "and the children of Israel walked upon dry land in the midst of the sea."

After this came that mysterious forty years of wandering in the desert which was planned and designed to purge the Israelites from the false teachings they had imbibed during their four hundred years of residence among the religions of Egypt.

If one again looks at any Old Testament map, one cannot help but remark how short the distance would have been had Moses led his people *directly across to Palestine*. Instead they were made to traverse the whole peninsula of Sinai before they were allowed to turn their faces toward the "Promised Land."

During that forty years of wandering a generation had passed away. Wisely and designedly the older race who had been contaminated by their long sojourn in Egypt had been "gathered to their fathers." Their place had been taken by the fresh blood of their sons and daughters, a younger generation more fitted to understand the teachings of the Great Law Giver—more fitted as "a chosen race," later on to hand down to posterity the pages of that Sacred Volume which was destined to illuminate and influence all races of mankind as well as their own.

It is this law of mysterious and wonderful Design that it is my privilege to draw attention to. It is more exemplified in the happenings and history of the Hebrew people than any other. If this race had been created for no other purpose than this, their sufferings and privations have not been in vain.

If I now proceed to demonstrate that the Divine Design I have so often alluded to may be found *even in the position of chapters and verses* in the Sacred Volume, I shall be doing nothing more than adding another proof to the many, that this inspired book is something so wonderful that it compels the veriest sceptic to believe in its Divine origin.

[1] Exodus xiv. 21.

In those far-off ages when Moses collected and put together the records of God's dealings with the children of Israel, the volume of the Sacred Law was not divided into chapters and verses.

Later still, David, the man who was specially chosen by God to be King of the Israelites, in writing the Psalms, could not by any natural means have surmised that when the Bible, some two thousand years after his death, came to be divided into chapters, the 119th Psalm would become *the longest chapter of the entire Book*, especially as scarcely one half of the Sacred Volume existed in his time.

This Psalm consists of 176 verses, every one of which directly or indirectly calls attention to the precepts laid down in the entire book.

The Psalm itself is, by some mysterious law of calculation, divided into 22 sections, *the exact number* of the letters that compose *the Hebrew alphabet*. Each section is subdivided into 8 verses, each verse being an iambic tetrameter, namely 16 syllables alternately short and long.[1]

Still more extraordinary is the fact that every one of the 8 verses of the first section begins with the first letter of the Hebrew alphabet: Aleph.

The 8 verses of the second section begin with the second letter of the Hebrew alphabet: Beth.

The 8 verses of the third section begin with the third letter of the alphabet: Gimel.

This extraordinary precision continuing until *all the 22 letters* of the Hebrew alphabet are employed.

When this wonderful chapter thousands of years later came to be translated into other languages, it was found that no other language could fit in with this rule. Therefore the Hebrew letters were set out simply as titles at the head of each of the eight sections, as may be seen if anyone looks up the 119th Psalm.

In the millions and millions of books that have been printed, there is *not one example in the world* of such an acrostic having ever been made, or of such an attempt having been thought of to call attention to the longest

[1] I am speaking, of course, of the Hebrew original version.

chapter of any work, especially when one considers that every verse of this chapter calls direct notice in one form or another to the good to be derived from following the precepts laid down in the volume of the Sacred Law.

Further, every verse alludes in some part of it to the Divine influence underlying the whole.

Example: The first verse contains the words "the law of the Lord."

2nd verse, "His testimonies."
3rd verse, "His ways."
4th verse, "Thy precepts."
5th verse, "Thy statutes."
6th verse, "Thy commandments."
7th verse, "Thy righteous judgments."
8th verse, "Thy statutes,"

and so on through the entire 22 sections.

The mystic number of 12 appears in the root words employed, which are Statutes, Ordinances, Faithfulness, Surety, Law, Name, Word, Precepts, Ways, Judgments, Testimonies, Commandments, and at least *one of these 12 words* are unerringly found in each of the 176 verses.

In the English version the two longest words employed are representative of the Bible, namely "Thy commandments" and "Thy testimonies." In their uses in this Psalm they present a strange coincidence with the 22 sections of the Psalm and the 22 letters of the original Hebrew alphabet. The word "commandments" is employed either in the singular or in the plural *exactly 22 times*, while "testimonies" is used 22 *times in the plural* and once in the singular at the end of the first half of the Psalm, namely the end of the 88th verse, which number *is itself a multiple of 22*.

To sum up, then, my observations on this, the most extraordinary example of *design* in literature written or printed that has ever been known. One cannot believe that such a thing could happen by chance; equally one cannot believe that some mortal, no matter how gifted, could have created a psalm in the form of an acrostic unmatched in the literature of the world, past or present;

still more so, that this psalm *should be designed* to be the longest chapter in a book *not then completed*.

And yet I have not exhausted all the features that call attention to this wonderful example of design.

It may not have been noticed before, by the many people who have read the Bible through from cover to cover, that both *the shortest* and the *longest chapters* of this wonderful book are placed *in close proximity to each other*, the shortest being the 117th and the longest the 119th Psalm. Now the one intermediary chapter between the shortest and the longest, the 118th, presents in itself such a number of remarkable coincidences that one is forced to the conclusion that these three psalms *were purposely planned* to come together for a definite reason—that reason evidently being that the relation of such coincidences would sooner or later strike some searcher of truth, as an illustration of Divine Design and consequently proof of the Divine Inspiration that guided not only the writer of the Psalms, but thousands of years later *the translators of this book into other languages*.

The 118th Psalm, occupying as it does the remarkable position of being between the shortest and longest chapters of the Bible, actually contains *the middle or central verse of the entire Bible*. This, the middle verse of the Sacred Book, is the 8th verse of the 118th Psalm.[1]

Its words are significant in their meaning—they are an epitome of the great truth taught all through the preceding chapters or those that follow: "It is better to trust in the Lord than to put confidence in man."

Further, if one writes down in figures Psalm 118, verse 8, and puts these numbers side by side, they become 1188, which is the *exact number of chapters in the Bible*, besides the one that contains the remarkable verse above quoted and which, as I called attention to before, *is the middle verse of the entire book*.

---

[1] The actual form and division of the Bible is the work of different minds, widely separated by time, by countries, and by training. There can therefore be no question of collusion in the carrying out of the evident design that underlies the construction of the Bible.

Next to this 118th Psalm, the 117th stands out as the shortest chapter of the Bible, and not only is this a curious fact, but it is still doubly so, by being at the same time *the central chapter* of the Book, having exactly *as many chapters before it as after it.*

The most accurate way of finding out if the 117th Psalm is the central chapter of the Bible is to refer to the table usually printed in the beginning of the Authorised Version. This table contains six columns or 39 books of the Old Testament and 27 books of the New. By adding together the numbers of chapters given by those six volumes we get the number 1189, the total number of the chapters in the Bible, the middle one must therefore be the 595th, as there cannot be anything else than 594 chapters before it and 594 following it.

The very number of 595, which is the number of the 117th Psalm, calculated as a chapter of the Bible, conveys in itself the idea of perfect symmetry, namely it can be read the same whether from left to right, or vice versa; it represents in itself *the principle of perfect equilibrium* which consists of equal disposition of the parts on both sides of a centre.

This, the shortest chapter in the Bible and the central one of the entire Book, has a striking significance of its own:

O praise the Lord all ye nations; praise Him all ye people. For His merciful kindness is great towards us: and the truth of the Lord endureth for ever.

One should not regard the extraordinary examples I have set out in these pages as isolated cases of mere coincidence, for when taken together, as they were evidently intended to be, they give the key to the construction of the Bible itself as a marvellous example of Divine inspiration. They tend to show that these three Psalms must have been written with a plan of forming these coincidences for some given purpose, and that the division and numeration of the entire Bible, so perfect in every way, *was prearranged* before even the greater part of it had been written by those who lived in later ages.

Surely this could only have been done by that Supreme Intelligence who so calculated and placed the millions of worlds revolving through space that they keep their appointed pathway through eternity to the smallest fraction of time.

In conclusion, in giving these examples of one of the many wonders of the Bible, I may have been permitted, in no matter how small a way, to stimulate interest in the Sacred Book itself.

To the many who have read it from cover to cover without noticing the mysterious examples it has been my privilege to call attention to, I can only hope that my words may encourage them to study it more deeply and find still greater truths for themselves.

While to those others—those of "little faith"—those who are longing to believe, but must have a "sign"—to these, I most humbly hope that the illustrations for which I have given them chapter and verse may be "the sign" for which they have been seeking—and in their new-found faith in the Divine Purpose underlying all things they may realise that form, number, and design are the expressions of that Infinite Mind "who works in a mysterious way, God's wonders to perform."

CHAPTER XXXIII

CONCLUSION

I TRUST my readers who have followed my theories through this book have grasped the fundamental fact underlying these pages, that the knowledge I have endeavoured to give to the public is of *a practical nature* with the decided object of helping my fellow men to make the best of themselves and render their lives as successful as possible.

Up to now occultism has been associated with the idea that its students must belong to the domain of dreamers of dreams, or those who live in some world of their own. In consequence of this idea the average "man in the street" has put aside such studies as not being useful, practical, or belonging to the money-making side of life.

It has also been drummed into his ears that all such studies bordered on witchcraft and were in some way or the other associated with the Devil.

Being brought up to go to church every Sunday and hearing every time he went that he was "a miserable sinner," doomed to punishment and torment both in this life and the world to come, he in the end believed that he was "a miserable sinner," and so dared not seek for any knowledge that might enable him to shake off the chains of conventionality and custom that ground him down and kept him in mental and intellectual slavery.

He had perhaps no means of knowing that some of the greatest kings of the world owed their success and wealth to advice given by their Astrologers, or that the Egyptian Magicians had greater power than either priest or potentate. He had perhaps never read that the great Queen Elizabeth consulted her astrologer and palmist, Dr. John Dee, on all important matters of State, and that the destiny of England had been guided from time to time by those students of occultism whom he had been taught to believe were but fit companions for black cats, and were workers of the Devil.

He had perhaps never read of that great English astrologer, William Lily, who had predicted the Fire of London *fifteen years before it took place*, or that the House of Commons had called him before that great assembly believing that, as he had predicted the calamity with such accuracy, he could explain to them what had caused such a catastrophe.

Further, his English History had never told him that Charles I had given the first thousand pounds his government sent him to Hampton Court to the same Lilly, the astrologer, asking him to predict his fate, and that had the King taken the warnings given to him by Astrology he might never have lost his head and descended to posterity as Charles the Martyr.

Again, it is probable he never knew that Queen Anne maintained an astrologer upon the roll of the Privy Purse, and that she had such faith in the celebrated Von Galgebrok that she asked him to predict the year of her death. This he did with perfect accuracy three years before the event, which took place on the 1st August, 1714.

* * * * *

Life is but the child of Mystery—we know not its origin—we know not its end. We see "as in a glass darkly" the threads of Destiny weaving the known and the unknown—and we wonder why.

We feel there is Design in all things—but it is only in looking back on the past that the wonders of "the pattern" become manifest.

We are indeed "of little faith," we children of men. We forget that we were made "in the image and likeness of God," and, in the forgetting, we have sold our birthright for "the mess of pottage" of man-made beliefs.

We do not dare to think for ourselves, for our "teachers" alone have wisdom? But alas! they locked the doors of knowledge, and the keys have rusted for want of use.

Behind all—the God of Patience—the God of Eternity—waits.

Slowly the ages pass: "A thousand years are but a day." Nations rise and fall. Teachers come and go. Time weaves Destiny into Design until in the end Perfection shines through the warp and weft and *the God-thought underlying all becomes manifest*.

If, then, one of the so-called "occult studies," such as I have tried to explain, has helped, in no matter how small a degree, to call attention to those hidden laws of life that illustrate the Divine Design, then when "the Call" comes —I will go my way, content that the years of study I have given to this work were not wasted and were not in vain.

*On the following pages are details of Arrow
books that will be of interest.*

THE BOOK OF CHINESE BELIEFS

Frena Bloomfield

Earth magic, ghost weddings, passports to the after-life: the spirit world of the Chinese exists side-by-side with everyday reality, and affects every aspect of Chinese life from diet and decor to getting married or opening a business.

Frena Bloomfield has lived and worked in Hong Kong and has talked in depth to many practitioners of the magic arts. *The Book of Chinese Beliefs* is a fascinating introduction to a rich culture where the dead are ever-present and even the siting of a house or village is governed by the laws of earth magic.

THE HANDBOOK OF CHINESE HOROSCOPES

Theodora Lau

Are you a sentimental but crafty Rat, a serious and dutiful Ox, or a captivating but unpredictable Tiger? Here, in the most comprehensive book ever written on Chinese astrology, you can find out which of the twelve animal signs of the lunar calendar is yours, how your sign is affected by the Yin and Yang, how your Moon sign and your Sun sign affect each other – and which of the other animal signs you're compatible with.

YOUR PSYCHIC WORLD A-Z
An everyday guide

Ann Petrie

Everyone is psychic.

Everyone has the ability to develop extrasensory perception, but few know what to do with it.

Taking examples from everyday life, this book looks at the efficiency of your energy and your love, and presents a whole new perspective on the psychic world.

It explains *why* certain unusual or uncanny situations occur, and how to handle them in ways most beneficial to you and those around you.

This guide tells you what to do if you — Meet a ghost, a ghoul or a poltergeist; Feel you've been cursed; Fall in love at first sight; Remember places you know you've never been to before; Have dreams that come true; Need to protect yourself from psychic attack — plus many more pieces of essential advice on relating to the psychic world around you.

Ann Petrie is a psychic-astrologer who combines her gifts in a unique way in writing, broadcasting and counselling.

BESTSELLING FICTION FROM ARROW

All these books are available from your bookshop or newsagent or you can order them direct. Just tick the titles you want and complete the form below.

☐	THE COMPANY OF SAINTS	Evelyn Anthony	£1.95
☐	HESTER DARK	Emma Blair	£1.95
☐	1985	Anthony Burgess	£1.75
☐	2001: A SPACE ODYSSEY	Arthur C. Clarke	£1.75
☐	NILE	Laurie Devine	£2.75
☐	THE BILLION DOLLAR KILLING	Paul Erdman	£1.75
☐	THE YEAR OF THE FRENCH	Thomas Flanagan	£2.50
☐	LISA LOGAN	Marie Joseph	£1.95
☐	SCORPION	Andrew Kaplan	£2.50
☐	SUCCESS TO THE BRAVE	Alexander Kent	£1.95
☐	STRUMPET CITY	James Plunkett	£2.95
☐	FAMILY CHORUS	Claire Rayner	£2.50
☐	BADGE OF GLORY	Douglas Reeman	£1.95
☐	THE KILLING DOLL	Ruth Rendell	£1.95
☐	SCENT OF FEAR	Margaret Yorke	£1.75
		Postage	_____
		Total	_____

ARROW BOOKS, BOOKSERVICE BY POST, PO BOX 29, DOUGLAS, ISLE OF MAN, BRITISH ISLES

Please enclose a cheque or postal order made out to Arrow Books Limited for the amount due including 15p per book for postage and packing both for orders within the UK and for overseas orders.

Please print clearly

NAME..

ADDRESS...

....

Whilst every effort is made to keep prices down and to keep popular books in print, Arrow Books cannot guarantee that prices will be the same as those advertised here or that the books will be available.